Not In *Our* Family !

by

Sherwood O. Cole, Ph.D.

Promise Publishing Co. Orange CA 92865

Not In Our Family!

by Sherwood O. Cole, Ph.D.

Library of Congress/Cataloging-in-Publication Data

Cole, Sherwood O.

Not In Our Family!

ISBN 0-939497-49-2

Dedication

To my wife, Dottie,

whose faith,

love

and friendship

inspire me.

About the Author

Sherwood Cole holds a B.A. degree in Psychology from the University of California at Santa Barbara, an M.A. in Psychology from the University of California, Los Angeles, and a Ph.D. in Psychology from Claremont Graduate School, also in California. Presently, he is Professor Emeritus of Psychology at Rutgers University where he taught for 26 years, as well as teaching part-time at the Rosemead School of Psychology at Biola University.

In addition to his years of teaching, he has published numerous articles on drug effects in professional journals and has presented papers at professional meetings. He is a member of the American Psychological Association and Society for Neuroscience as well as being a Fellow of the Royal Society of Health in England.

Acknowledgments

First and foremost, I thank my wife, Dottie, for her encouragement in writing this book and for her many hours spent at the computer in editing and re-writing. During times of discouragement and disillusionment over the apathy of the Christian community regarding drug issues, she has been a stalwart supporter of this project. Without her support and encouragement, this book would not have become a reality.

Secondly, I thank my colleagues at Biola University for their many suggestions and recommendations. I am particularly indebted to Dr. J. P. Moreland who provided feedback on an earlier version of this book. Such feedback has enabled me to think through some issues with much greater clarity. I am also grateful to the administration of Rosemead School of Psychology (Dr. Patricia Pike, Dean) for scheduling my part-time teaching load in such a manner as to maximize my free time for writing.

Lastly, I thank Mary Belle Steele of Promise Publishing Company for her editorial expertise. Her recommendations and changes in the final draft of my book have minimized my idiosyncratic shortcomings and greatly improved the readability of the book.

Table of Contents

Preface

In today's society, Christian parents, youth workers and pastors must be concerned about how they can most effectively address the problem of drug use and abuse among our young people. It is quite apparent that simply providing our young people with drug information by itself, or encouraging their mass participation in drug-prevention programs (e.g., the current D.A.R.E. program) does not give them sufficient protection. In many such instances, drug information simply makes for a more sophisticated drug user and reduces the perceived dangers of using drugs. It is also the case that drug-prevention contracts are only as good as the moral character of the young person and are frequently abandoned in the heat of peer pressure and the need for social acceptance. General scare tactics as a strategy for encouraging young people to avoid drugs are equally shallow in substance and they frequently backfire on well-intentioned adults.

While drug information has its place and can be a valuable instrument if used properly, all of the secular strategies mentioned above lack the most important ingredient in any drug-prevention program—a moral basis. For those of us who are Christians, the Bible and its principles provide such a moral basis and, when further combined with critical drug information, yields a sound strategy for addressing the problems of drug use and abuse. This book attempts to provide such a balanced view of biblical principles and drug information in the hope that parents, youth workers and pastors will have the appropriate tools to prepare our young people as they are forced to cope with the drugs so prevalent in our communities and schools today.

The information in these chapters is not be construed in any manner, or to any degree to be a substitute for medical advice.

Several specific features have been incorporated into the format of the book to facilitate its usefulness to the reader. They are as follows:

- The nature of the growing drug problem among Christian young people and the reasons for such a problem (see chapters 1 and 2).

- The book is divided into two general sections—biblical guidelines (chapters 3-9) and drug information (chapters 10-13). An attempt has been made to keep the account of drug information as non-technical and readable as possible. If the reader desires more specific information on drug action, principles and classificiation, such information is provided in the appendices (A, B and C).

- Chapters 1-9 begin with a real-life drug problem appropriate to the discussion of the chapter. These examples represent a composite of actual experiences brought to the attention of the author; however, the names have been changed to protect the individuals involved. It is hoped that such practical examples will help the reader tie the content of the chapter to real life.

- Chapters 3-13 are followed by specific questions that have been answered in the context of the chapter. It is hoped that such a format will increase the user-friendly qualities of the book, and encourage the readers to review and highlight those portions of greatest interest to them.

I trust that this book will be of help to all Christians concerned about the growing drug epidemic in our society. God bless you—and good reading!

Chapter One

So, What's The Problem?

Judy was adopted by Christian parents at the age of two and was accustomed to attending church and Sunday School on a regular basis. While in elementary school, she made a profession of faith in Christ and was subsequently baptized (sprinkled) in the Presbyterian Church. While she had demonstrated behavioral problems in elementary school (actually being diagnosed as hyperactive), she became particularly difficult to manage in high school. At the encouragement of her peers in junior ROTC, she began to experiment with a variety of illicit drugs. She was reasonably successful in keeping such experiences from her parents by avoiding close encounters with them.

During the summer between her sophomore and junior years of high school, Judy ran away from home on several occasions for a period of several days at a time. During these times her parents had no idea where she was or what she was doing, although they later learned that she had been heavily into drugs and sleeping out of doors in tents with some of her friends (both males and females). Although Judy was eventually able to complete her high school education in an "alternative program," she distanced herself from her parents as much as possible and continued to use drugs with her friends.

Judy's parents were in total shock and disbelief that such a thing could happen to their family and they were ill-equipped to deal with it. After all, their home was a Christian home and things like this are not supposed to happen in such an environment. Drug abuse occurs in non-Christian homes where family values and biblical principles are not taught ... at least, this is what they believed, as do many Christian parents.

Fortunately for Judy and her parents this is not the end of the story. She was eventually able to get her life back on track with the help of an in-house drug rehabilitation program and professional counseling.

I find a basic lack of interest in drug-related problems and issues among Christians, in general, and Christian parents, in particular. As a result, they are totally unprepared and unequipped to deal with such problems when it becomes necessary to do so. As is true with society in general, Christians are so busy with their stressed lifestyle that they have neither the time nor the inclination to confront such problems, unless their own families have been touched by some drug-related tragedy. Even then, as was true with Judy's parents, solutions may not be readily available or apparent. Even those parents who have the time and inclination to confront such problems need someone trained in the biological sciences to help them make sense out of the information related to drug effects, addiction and similar issues. After all, if we're forced into making tough decisions, we must inform ourselves in order to make reasonably good ones.

As Christians, we believe that "the Bible provides us with what we need in tough times," but this reminds me of an experience I had while in graduate school. One of my fellow students named Bill, knowing I was a Christian, asked me, "If Christ is the answer, what is the question?" At first, I was offended by this apparent attack on my faith, but the more I thought about it, the more I realized the question was not only reasonable, but it deserved an answer.

Christ is the only answer in regard to man's lost condition and spiritual need. But, when we say, "The Bible is our answer to tough drug questions," it must be given the acid test of specific application. What specific drug problem or issue are you talking about and what does the Bible have to say (by example or teaching) concerning that specific issue?

Christians can find the tools to answer their questions in regard to drug issues, and here we hope to provide a clear biblical framework for interpreting and applying drug information to real life situations. An impossible task, you say! No, but most certainly a challenging one.

There is a general apathy of the Christian community in regard to the problem of drug abuse and there are some underlying reasons for such indifference. There are some specific reasons why young people misuse and abuse drugs. There is specific drug information available, and, best of all, there are specific biblical guidelines for dealing with drug problems. Fasten your mental seat belt, for the road may be challenging at times.

The Need For A Wake-up Call

Recently, I offered a course on Christian solutions to drug abuse as an adult Sunday School elective in an evangelical church. I anticipated throngs of young married couples with school-age children clamoring to get into the course so that they might learn more about this timely issue. To my amazement, there was, instead, a kind of general apathy among the congregation to the topic, and those who did attend seemed to me to be the ones who least needed the information.

Just before the course began, Tom and Betty (a prominent church couple) proceeded to inform me that they would not be attending the course because they "don't do drugs". The confrontational nature of their statement was somewhat amazing to me. Comments made by other married couples with children were similar in nature, although they tended to be communicated in more subtle terms. Not only did there appear to be a general indifference to such a course, but I got the impression that the mere offering of such a course in an evangelical church was perceived by some members of the congregation as an affront to Bible-believing Christians. Apparently, Christians see drug abuse as somebody else's problem, not ours. Unfortunately, such an attitude only reflects the need for a reality check. This is a problem affecting church young people in increasing numbers.

The fact is that the problem of drug abuse is no longer simply out there in the secular world but it is also flourishing in our Christian homes and churches. Drug abuse is no longer simply knocking at the door of our sanctuaries, but it has, in fact, gained a strong foothold in many segments of the Christian community.

A 1991 *Christianity Today* article reported that, by the time Christian teenagers graduate from high school, 57% of them will have tried an illicit (illegal) drug. Furthermore, 17% of those in this group will have tried cocaine or crack cocaine, one of the most dangerous drugs on the market today.[1] My discussions with college-age Christian young people over the last few years would suggest that these statistics are conservative estimates and that, by the time they are ready for college, a larger percentage will have experimented with various drugs.

While the general level of drug abuse (including alcohol abuse) among churched young people is still less than it is among their secular, non-churched counterparts, the gap is rapidly closing.[2] In all likelihood, this gap will continue to narrow and, in the next five to ten years, we will see an increase in the kind of drug-related tragedies in the Christian community that have, for many years, characterized the secular world of drug abuse. The latest available information further indicates an increase in the use of marijuana by 8th and 10th graders in 1996,[3] and there is good reason to believe that Christian as well as non-Christian teenagers have contributed to these findings.

A Campus Life magazine survey also reported that 45% of religious-oriented students claim to drink alcoholic beverages.[4] Admittedly, the degree of alcohol consumption varied markedly (seldom, once a week, occasionally); however, this figure is still astounding considering the fact that the survey was circulated among students from a largely evangelical, conservative background. Normally, one would consider such a background as one of the primary reasons for abstaining from the use of alcohol—at least in the past, that was a reasonable assumption. Apparently, there is a serious gap in the lives of many young Christians between their stated beliefs and religious convictions and the degree to which such factors have a serious impact on their behavior.

Part of the problem with the use of alcohol among Christian young people is the fact that social drinking has become more acceptable among Christians in general, even evangelicals.[5] While evangelicals used to be characterized as teetotalers, this distinction no longer holds. Nearly two-thirds of Protestants now admit to drinking socially[6] and the impact of such behavior on young people cannot be minimized. Alcohol is as much a drug as any other chemical substance and merely separating it from other drugs of abuse (as is sometimes done by authors) does not change the picture in any manner.

While the evidence for drug use among Christian young people is startling, it does not convey the tragedy and pain caused in the Christian home of drug-abusing teenagers and their families. Only stories like Judy's (shared at the beginning of the chapter) can do that.

In light of the overwhelming evidence for the invasion of drug abuse into the Christian community, it would seem that there really is a serious need for a wakeup call to all Christians. If we don't wake up to the reality of drug abuse within the Christian community, it may soon be too late to do much about it. Furthermore, how we deal with this serious matter may be one of the most critical decisions made by the Christian community in this century.

While the development of recovery-group ministries found in some of the more progressive churches is certainly a step in the right direction,[7] such programs tend to be "closet" ministries serving the broader community. Members of the congregation are seldom aware of what goes on in these programs and in many instances, they choose not to be involved in them for a variety of reasons. Until the entire Christian community can be challenged, the problem of drug abuse will never be addressed adequately.

Why Are Christians Blind to the Drug Problem?

There is no easy or simple answer to this question. A number of factors probably contribute to the indifference of the Christian community to the problem of drug abuse. Let's examine these factors in some detail.

- There appears to be widespread ignorance of the nature and extent of the problem of drug abuse.

In many instances, this ignorance may simply be characterized by a naiveté on the part of some Christians to contemporary problems and issues in general. Not only are these individuals uninformed about drug problems within the Christian community but they are equally uninformed about other social and moral issues confronting the body of believers. Perhaps, nothing short of a major drug-related disaster hitting their home or church would serve as an effective wakeup call. It would also appear that such general ignorance is not limited to members of the congregation, but may also include many pastors. For example, while most pastors recognize that there is a problem of drug abuse among young people, a survey indicated that only 13% felt that there was a serious problem in their own church.[8] One wonders whether the doors of these pastors' studies will have to be kicked down before they realize that their young people are having to deal with this problem. Hopefully, not.

However, I am convinced that in many other instances, ignorance of drug problems within the Christian community is the result of a more active stance and not simply due to the more passive role of naiveté. These Christians are ignorant of drug problems because that's the way they want it to be; ignorance provides them with a comfort zone within which to run their lives. After all, if you are unaware of the drug problem, you don't have to deal with it.

Such an attitude reminds me of a conversation I had many years ago with an older, well-entrenched Christian named Ruth.

While I was challenging some of her beliefs, which was intended to be constructive in nature and to help her think through her faith, the whole process back-fired miserably. At one point, I was simply told, "I know what I believe, so don't confuse me with any more facts." Ruth's message was loud and clear. While, over the years, I have become more sensitive and respectful of other people's comfort zone, her response made a lasting impression on me. Unfortunately, many Christians have a similar attitude regarding the need to know about drug problems. Such knowledge is too intrusive and will, undoubtedly, rock their comfort zone.

- Another reason for the complacency of the Christian community to the problems of drug abuse may be the fear of accepting blame and guilt.

If, in your complacency, you let yourself believe that the drug problem isn't real or, at least, that it isn't that serious, then there is no reason to experience guilt. If, however, there really is a problem, someone must assume responsibility for it, and who is in a better position to do so than parents? Parents sometimes play the "*If-only-I-had-done-this*" game, which is an exercise in futility and seldom leads to constructive change.[9] While all parents have occasionally done this, we must guard against the inherent dangers in such a practice. If not dealt with realistically, such experiences can immobilize the individual and seriously affect one both spiritually and psychologically.

- A third and final reason for the complacency of the Christian community to the problem of drug abuse may be the fear of rejection.

Everyone wants to be accepted by their peers and friends, and this is no different in the Christian community. Recently, I was talking to Maria (a young Latino woman) who had a friend struggling with the problem of substance abuse. While her friend had made a profession of faith in Christ, she was, nevertheless, continuing to struggle with this problem of abuse. Maria was telling me how her friend had sought advice and support from another Christian, only to be told that she couldn't possibly be a

Christian in light of such a problem and that her abuse was a clear indication of demonic influences in her life. That gave Maria's friend a strong sense of rejection by a fellow Christian which, in turn, produced a fear of also being rejected by other Christians she might turn to for help. Now, she only seeks help with her abuse problem through secondary sources. Maria was, apparently, one of the few people this friend could trust with her problem.

While I tried to assure Maria that not all Christians would react that way and that professional help was available for her friend, I wonder how many other Christians are keeping their problems of drug abuse to themselves in fear of being misunderstood, criticized or rejected by fellow Christians.

The reticence of Christians to share their problem of drug abuse creates a false sense of everything being all right and contributes to the complacency of the Christian community toward the problems of drug abuse. The parents of Judy (mentioned at the beginning of the chapter) did not seek help from their pastor or other church members because they, too, felt that they would be misunderstood, criticized or rejected by their friends at church. All too often, this sense of rejection is real, not just imaginary.

Many Christians are convinced that good parenting guarantees good children and that children with problems of drug abuse reflect the failure of such parents in raising their children. However, God's Word on this matter (Prov. 22:6) should be viewed as a principle of truth rather than an invariable rule. Generally, good parents do produce good children, but there are exceptions to this principle, even in Christian families.

The role that *ignorance, guilt,* and *rejection* play in the apathy of the Christian community toward the problem of drug abuse is a head-in-the-sand approach to solving problems. We tend to forget that, while our head is in the sand, the rest of us is fully exposed to all of the consequences of our surroundings. Whether we recognize it or not, the problem of drug abuse in the Christian community is going to have an impact on our lives and the lives of our children. Therefore, it is time for the Christian community to take the proverbial "bull by the horns" and do something about the problem while time is still on our side. To wait until tomorrow to do something about a problem that has already established a strong foothold in our midst may be the classical error of offering too little, too late. As individual Christians, we need to equip ourselves for the battle on drug abuse and go on the offensive.

How Do We Prepare for the War on Drugs?

Christian parents, workers, and pastors can do a lot to prepare themselves for the war on drugs by following two simple principles—both of which have a sound scriptural basis.

The first principle is this: to study and apply the many scriptural guidelines for dealing with problems of both drug use and abuse. In this regard, we are reminded that: *All Scripture is given by inspiration of God, and is profitable for doctrine, for correction, for instruction in righteousness* (II Tim. 3:16, KJV).

It is true that Scripture is given to be a guide to our relationship with God through His Son, Jesus Christ. However, since the spiritual truths of Scripture are couched in the context of real people and their experiences, we are able to learn a great deal about the application of spiritual truths to real-life situations. While it is true that the culture of biblical times is markedly different from our present culture, the people and their struggles are not that different. Part of this struggle had to do with the use and abuse of various kinds of herbal drugs.

As we will see in later chapters, the Bible teaches, by command and example, the proper use of drugs as well as the consequences of their abuse. Why does the Bible provide us with such practical examples? It does so that we might be thoroughly equipped to live righteous lives (II Tim. 3:17)—this means righteous living as it relates to drug issues as well as other areas of our lives.

The second principle is this: to become better informed about drugs. Learn as much as you can about the drugs that are being abused by our young people. Find out as much as you can about the side effects and dangers of such drugs. We are again reminded to: *Study to shew thyself approved unto God, a workman that needeth not to be ashamed, rightly dividing the Word of truth* (II Tim. 2:15, KJV).

Of course, this passage focuses primarily on the study and application of God's Word, but, in principle, it also refers to study in general. Far too often, Christians have been encouraged to leave their thinking caps at the door or to turn off our minds. We're likely to be told by well-meaning Christians to trust in the Lord and everything will work out. God's promise of the Holy Spirit guiding us into all truth (John 16:13) is not given to empty-headed Christians, particularly those who are that way by choice. Instead, God expects us to maximize our intelligence and mental faculties by bringing them under the influence of the Holy Spirit. Some Christians (hopefully not very many) see the acquisition of practical knowledge and the application of reason as an affront to their faith rather than a buttress to it.

This should not be the case, particularly with a problem such as drug abuse which has the potential for destroying the very foundation of our Christian lifestyle. Many Christians are strapped for time and acquiring information about drugs requires considerable sacrifice. Still, any information about drugs is better than none and could make a significant difference in the response you make to a drug-related crisis at some point in the future.

This book is designed to give you a start in this task, but may need to be supplemented by additional sources.[10] If you do not find what you need in some published form, ask a person whom you trust and who is likely to be knowledgeable on the subject—perhaps a physician or pharmacist friend. The important thing is to make some effort to become informed. May the Spirit of God guide you into truth, wherever and in whatever form it is found, and provide you with a solid foundation for dealing with the problem of drug abuse within our Christian community.

Notes

Chapter Two

Why Do Young People Abuse Drugs?

Chris graduated from a Christian high school and found it relatively easy to maintain a Christian testimony while there. Although he heard rumors that a few of the male students in the high school had experimented with drugs, he personally was unscathed by such exposure. Moreover, Chris had come to the personal conviction that drugs had no place in his Christian life if he hoped to maintain any kind of witness to fellow students. He was not haughty or condemning in his attitude toward other students who might be using drugs; rather, he had simply decided that he would not become a victim of such slavery.

However, Chris had a new challenge. He was a freshman at a large Eastern University and living in the dormitory with classmates who were predominantly worldly in their outlook. He found the pressures to conform to their non-Christian standards to be extremely powerful and occasionally wondered whether giving in a little bit to such pressures might be something he could live with. He talked to his parents by phone about his situation and prayed that the Lord would give him wisdom and strength to make the right decision. After much agonizing and prayer, he decided to stick by his convictions and to remain drug free regardless of the personal cost. Such a decision was not easy since the majority of his classmates drank beer and smoked pot in their dormitory rooms on a fairly regular basis. The fact that it was against University policy to do so was of little concern to them.

While Chris was initially ridiculed and made fun of for his stand, some of his fellow classmates eventually began to develop a genuine respect and affection for him. About that time, Chris became acquainted with two other Christians who were living in the same dormitory and began to meet with them on a regular basis for Bible study and prayer. While the other two Christians had occasionally shared a beer with their classmates in order to be accepted, they were so impressed by Chris' stand that they, too, decided to give up drinking. Before the school year was over, Chris and his two friends established a strong Christian witness in their dormitory.

We can all rejoice at Chris' story and be thankful that his stand against drugs was an essential part of his Christian testimony. Unfortunately and sadly, however, Chris' story is the exception, not the rule, among Christian young people. More and more, Christian young people are giving in to the secular pressures of drug abuse.

The first question that comes to mind is, "Do Christian and non-Christian young people abuse drugs for the same reasons?" If they do, then, what has happened to the impact of traditional Christian values on our young people? If they don't, then, we need to identify the unique influences within the Christian community that lead to such choices. As we look for answers to these questions, I believe that you may be surprised and shocked.

In thirty-plus years of experience in higher education, I have had the privilege of teaching and interacting with students in both Christian and secular contexts. This experience has allowed me to observe the changes that have taken place over the years in both of these settings. My early experience in two Christian colleges (1961-1966) gave me a strong sense of what was unique about Christian education and the general atmosphere of a Christian college campus. Quite typically, students were required not only to sign a statement of faith and practice, but they conducted themselves in ways that distinguished them clearly from their secular counterparts. Their dress code, their taste in music and entertainment, and the content of their conversations all distinguished them as a unique and special segment of society. I well remember when the question of whether Christian young people should go to movies or not was the hottest topic of debate on many Christian campuses.

My many subsequent years of experience in a secular university (1966-1992) quickly taught me that things were very different in the outside world. The secular university prides itself in being on the cutting edge of social and political change, and I found this pride to be generally justified. However, such a cutting edge posture usually meant giving up traditional interests and standards and giving in to the liberal trends of society. Over the twenty-six years I was at this secular university, I saw a general tolerance for the Judeo-Christian world view gradually lose ground, eventually being replaced by the causes of special interest groups. I wasn't terribly surprised by these changes, since they merely reflected what was going on in our society at large.

My surprise came in returning to Christian education. I was totally unprepared for what I found and am still attempting to make adjustments to the changes that have taken place on Christian college campuses. Young people no longer dress differently than their secular counterparts, their interest in music and entertainment is very similar to non-Christians, and it's hard to tell how the content of their conversations in the college coffee shop differs from those heard on any college campus.

Furthermore, it's not only a matter of change in external appearance, for students in Christian colleges are challenging the traditional standards of abstinence from alcohol and tobacco.[1] The argument is that these prohibitions are merely attempts to control and modify their behavior and that, at some point in their lives, young Christians must make decisions about such matters on their own. Why not make such decisions in the caring, supportive environment of a Christian college campus? In all fairness, most students are still willing to honor the code of conduct required of such colleges and there is a noticeable absence of discarded cigarette butts and beer cans around campus. However, these changes in lifestyles and attitudes of students on Christian college campuses are highly significant and not to be taken lightly.

What in the world has happened to Christian education and Christian college campuses? Have they lost their distinctiveness and calling as a unique form of education and experience? The answer is, to some degree, yes. While most of the same Bible and theology courses are taught and the Christian world view is still the prevailing philosophy, the lifestyle of Christian students has changed dramatically. This secularization of the Christian lifestyle is only reflective of the broader changes going on in our churches and Christian community at large. However, it is of special importance in the lives of our young people.

After this brief history of changes in education, one might ask, "What is the relevance of these changes in regard to why young people abuse drugs?" The relevance is this—with the increased secularization of Christian college campuses and our young people, differences in the reason for abusing drugs become less clear and may disappear altogether. Christian young people abuse drugs for many of the same reasons that their secular counterparts abuse drugs.

Drug Use Versus Drug Abuse

The distinction between use and abuse is commonly made on the basis of degree of drug involvement. If someone is taking a drug in a controlled manner or in a small amount, this would most likely be called drug use. In this case, taking a prescription drug or even experimenting with or taking illegal drugs for occasional, recreational purposes would be considered drug use. On the other hand, when one becomes compulsive in one's attitude and action about drugs, this would properly be considered drug abuse. In this case, the person's lifestyle is oriented around obtaining and taking the drug on a daily basis, usually in increasingly larger amounts. Such drug abuse is characterized not only by harmful effects on the individual abuser but also on the lives of others around them.[2]

While such a distinction may have some practical value, it is often difficult to know at what stage the behavior becomes abusive. The transition from one stage to the other is gradual and progressive and may go totally unnoticed by the non-professional observer. When drug use becomes misuse (behavior patterns change or become more intense), this should be a clear warning sign that the potential for drug abuse is very real. Since individuals differ markedly in their reaction to drugs, it is also important to keep in mind that what may be drug use for one person may constitute drug abuse for another.

The business man who has two cocktails with lunch each day may be totally unaffected by such a practice. However, the infrequent drinker or someone who has difficulty metabolizing alcohol may be devastated by such behavior. In the latter case, it would probably be appropriate to refer to the behavior as abusive, although the degree of drug involvement is still relatively small.

What this discussion about drug use and abuse lacks more than anything else is a moral framework for its distinctions. Drug abuse is not only harmful and even life-threatening, it is also morally wrong. While drug use may not be as harmful as abusive behavior, it, too, is wrong when it encourages a sustained pattern of involvement with any drug or if it includes the use of illegal drugs. Thus, morally, the distinction between the improper use of any drug and drug abuse becomes moot. Our Christian standards in dealing with drug issues must include such moral judgment. Scripture reminds us that Christian wisdom is different from worldly wisdom (I Cor. 2:5-8) and that we are not to conform to the patterns of the world (Rom. 12:2).

Reasons Why Young People Abuse Drugs

Any attempt to list the reasons for drug abuse tends to point out our ignorance on the subject. In all likelihood, the reasons for drug abuse among young people (as well as other age groups) is as varied as are the individuals. Any attempt to discuss this issue must, out of necessity, deal in generalities and be incomplete. With this in mind, the following factors are viewed as potential contributors to drug abuse.

Genetic factors, while not specifically causing drug abuse, may predispose someone to such behavior.[3] This does not mean that they will automatically become abusers but, merely, that there is a greater likelihood that they will develop such behavior. Studies which control for environmental influences, indicate that children of alcoholic parents (particularly sons of alcoholic fathers) have a much higher prospect of becoming alcoholics themselves. It is possible that this increased risk is the result of differences in brain activity of pre-alcoholic sons. It is also possible that genetic factors contribute to chemical differences which cause alcoholics to metabolize alcohol differently than non-alcoholics.

One characteristic that seems to be common to all alcoholics is their ability to drink more than other people. This observation suggests that alcoholics metabolize alcohol more rapidly than non-alcoholics and that such a difference in metabolic activity may be inherited. While alcoholics may start drinking for the same reasons as anyone else, they end up being trapped by predisposing, biological factors that have their roots in genetics.

Undoubtedly, another factor that may contribute to drug abuse is **social-cultural influences.** Some young people abuse drugs because they choose to identify with a deviant subcultural group.[4] Within such a group, the use or abuse of a particular drug may not only be tolerated, but may be expected as part of a ritualistic requirement for membership. Still others may abuse drugs because of peer pressure or the desire to impress their friends.

Many young people also take drugs to have a good time with their peers. In such a case, the motive is clearly social in nature. So called "gateway drugs" (alcohol and cigarettes) probably introduce many young people to the social pressures of peer conformity. Once the social pressures are in place, young people often move on to abuse more powerful, illegal drugs.

While parents may think they continue to have a significant influence over their teenage children, evidence suggests that, in general, peer influence is more important. When parent and peer influence are in the same direction (assuming that such influences are positive), we should be thankful for such an occurrence. More common, however, is the case where parents oppose drug use but peer pressure encourages such behavior, creating a serious conflict. Parents must recognize that peer pressure is likely to win out in such a conflict.

Another reason for drug abuse might simply be a **rebellious attitude** and **desire to impress others.**[5] Many teenagers seem to enjoy impressing people, including their parents and other adults. It's not always easy for young people to get the attention of adults, and drug abuse (as well as other forms of deviant behavior) is one way of accomplishing that. The means of getting their attention is not as important as the fact that they have accomplished their objective. In fact, the means can be pretty bizarre or disgusting at times, particularly when drug abuse is combined with other visual reminders of rebellion such as outrageous hairdos and tattoos. Hopefully, parents will not lose sight of the critical nature of drug abuse in such brazen displays of rebellion.

Although somewhat controversial, certain **personality traits** may also contribute to the problem of drug abuse.[6] However, one has to be careful not to make the mistake of assuming that all abusers are simply weak individuals, and therefore, vulnerable to drugs. Rather, a variety of affective and personality disorders may attract individuals to drugs as a means of coping with the disorder. It appears that such personality traits as high emotionality, anxiety, low frustration tolerance, low self-esteem, compulsiveness, depression, hostility and the inability to adapt to change may make an individual more vulnerable to drug abuse.

Our young people are under tremendous pressures these days and the possibility of such pressures influencing personality characteristics, and in turn increasing vulnerability to drugs, cannot be overlooked. However, an additional word of caution would seem to be appropriate, since the expression of such traits may be the **result** of drug abuse as well as the **cause** of such behavior. In spite of the potential role of personality traits in drug abuse, it would seem premature to assume that there is such a thing as a true addictive personality.

Perhaps, the most important reason for drug abuse is the **effect of the drug** itself.[7] Many young drug abusers may be seeking some deviation from their mundane day-to-day experiences. Psychoactive drugs produce an altered state of consciousness and permit the individual to perceive the world in a different and more exciting way. For many young people, such an escape from reality is an appealing break from the pressures of teenage competition and is capable of reinforcing a particular pattern of abusive behavior.

Both Christian and non-Christian young people seem to be caught up in a desire for more and more excitement. Those of us who are adults have the clear impression that it takes a lot more to excite young people today than it did when we were kids. Because young people quickly adapt to such excitement, it appears that they continue to need greater amounts of arousal to keep them satisfied. As a result, they choose new and more daring experiences to meet that need. Activities that progressively increase the experience of excitement are appropriately referred to by one author as "the acceleration syndrome".[8] Since many drugs provide a quick, easy way of changing mood, drug abuse among young people is a natural consequence of such a syndrome.

Not only does such a syndrome encourage the general use of drugs by young people but, because of the increased need for excitement, the syndrome may encourage them to seek out stronger and stronger drug effects. The drugs that were previously effective are no longer effective and, now, must be replaced by more powerful and highly addictive drugs. It's no wonder that the powerful psychological effects of drugs has such a hold on the minds of our young people—Christian and non-Christian alike.

Social-cultural Roots Of Drug Abuse

Many of us are old enough to remember the counter-cultural movement of the 1960's. This was the time of hang-loose ethics and a rejection of many of the values and practices that defined the very core of our society. To live and let live was the prevailing philosophy of the day and young people expressed their individualism by how they dressed, behaved, and thought.[9] The cry of these "hippies" (a term with which they became identified) was to experience yourself and the world in new ways. Drug abuse became a common practice during this period and was seen as the primary means of acquiring this new perspective on life. Gurus of the hippy movement (Timothy Leary, Harvard professor and Ken Kesey, celebrated author) encouraged further experimentation with such drugs and set the agenda for the movement's spiritual enlightenment emphasis.[10] While interests in the hippy movement faded in the 1970's, its impact on our society is still being felt today.

If you ask, "Where are the hippies of the 60's and 70's today," the answer might surprise you. The reason is that the hippies of that era are still with us but have undergone a transformation that allowed them to re-establish themselves in main-stream society. The hippies of the 60's and 70's became the "yuppies" of the 1980's and are now prominent figures in business and industry.[11] Surprised? Well, don't be. While this re-absorption back into society is equally as impressive as the counter-cultural movement of the 60's and 70's, it has been accompanied by far less fanfare.

Although many of the trends of the 60's and 70's have disappeared with the cultural re-absorption of supporters, one trend has not—that of drug abuse. The drug abuse that was so prevalent at that time has not waned and continues to plague our society in an even more pervasive manner. Furthermore, many of the current drug problems can be directly traced to the practice of drug use during this earlier counter-cultural movement. As Morey has aptly pointed out:

> Though the psychedelic sixties and partying seventies are but memories, drugs have endured into the nineties. They are now considered a vital part of certain Eastern religious or occult practices which have recently taken Western society by storm.[12]

Such a lasting impact of the 60's and 70's cannot be ignored and, undoubtedly, is one of the underlying reasons for the wide-spread abuse of drugs in today's society. Hopefully, as Christians we can find ways to dissociate ourselves from this trend and discover our own effective ways of dealing with the problem.

Spiritual Roots Of Drug Abuse

While all of the preceding factors are important, they overlook one very important characteristic of human nature—its self-centeredness. This self-centeredness is particularly prevalent during the teenage years since this is the period during which one develops a self image and a concept of self-esteem. Drug abuse tends to be self-centered behavior in that the individual is more concerned about satisfying his or her own desires than those of others.

From a Christian perspective, self-centeredness (and by implication, drug abuse) is the result of a person's sinful nature. While biological, psychological and social explanations of drug abuse have their place and help us to understand the nature of the drug problem, sin ultimately underlies all of our problems. The failure to recognize human depravity as the root of the problem can lead to some ill-fated attempts at correcting it. However, looking at drug abuse in this manner encourages one to seek answers to the problem from God's Word. That's what we are going to do.

With the secularization of the Christian community, it may be getting increasingly difficult for Christian young people to make the important distinctions between sinful and acceptable practices. Many Christian young people appear to view "living under grace" as a license to experiment with a variety of secular practices, including experimenting with drugs. It's quite possible that such an attitude is further reinforced by the behavior of their parents or other members of the Christian community. However, Paul warns us about such a callous attitude regarding our position in the Lord (Rom. 6:14-15). We are not to abuse our position under grace; we are to be servants unto righteousness.

It may be difficult to convince some Christian young people that it is not okay for them to abuse drugs when they see their non-Christian friends doing it. However, if we don't help them to see the self-serving and destructive nature of such practices, we fail them miserably. At that point, not only have our young people lost any sense of the uniqueness of the Christian life, but we have also lost such a perspective. Hopefully, this will not happen.

Notes

Part One

Biblical Guidelines

Chapter Three

Drugs in the Bible

Tim grew up in a Christian home and was familiar with all of the Bible stories for children. "Noah's Ark," "David and Goliath," and "Daniel in the Lion's Den" were old stuff to him, and he was repeatedly told by his parents that such stories reflect the principles by which Christians are to live. "Believe in God's power and trust Him in times of need," was the family's motto ever since he could remember. God's Word and its teachings were the cornerstone of his family life.

Tim accepted the Lord in a church youth meeting and was excited about exploring the opportunities available in Christian service. Through a contact made at school, Tim was able to arrange a summer job as a carpenter, a skill he thought he might be able to use on a short-term mission project in the future. Unfortunately, the adult Tim worked with was not a Christian and, after much persuasion, he convinced Tim that smoking a "joint" was no more harmful than puffing on a cigarette.

While Tim had been well coached on the dangers of cigarette smoking, he saw smoking one joint as no big deal. However, one joint became a regular practice, and he was soon hooked on marijuana. When the summer came to an end, Tim realized he had a serious problem and had to deal with it head on. He knew from what his parents taught him that the Bible had all the answers to his spiritual problems, but what about his drug problem? He didn't recall anything ever being said about drugs in the Bible or people in biblical times having problems with drugs. Even if the Bible did say something about drugs (he remembered that wine was mentioned in the Bible), it happened so long ago, what possible relevance could it have to the kind of problem he faced now? He was sure that he would have to look elsewhere for help. Fortunately, Tim eventually found the help he needed through a Christian friend.

Tim's dilemma is a common one among Christians; while convinced that Scripture is our guide in spiritual matters, many believe the Bible is out-of-date regarding other areas of our life and has little or nothing to say regarding practical matters. This, of course, is not true. However, Scripture may require us to dig deep for guidelines in dealing with other areas of our life. It is with such a perspective that the present chapter attempts to demonstrate the relevance of Scripture to contemporary drug problems.

We may think that drug problems are unique to our times; however, evidence suggests that drug use and abuse have always been part of recorded human history. Ancient societies used psychoactive drugs that were contained in a wide variety of plant species. Archaeological evidence suggests that the use of the drug opium (obtained from the opium poppy) may go back as far as 4,000 B. C. and that the Egyptians were familiar with its potential medical uses as well as with its psychoactive properties.[1] Sumerian tablets and Greek writings of this early period (4,000-1,000 B. C.) also suggest widespread knowledge about the euphoric and addictive properties of opium. Egyptian records from about 1,500 B. C. list numerous additional herbal compounds and the drinking of alcohol, a practice that, undoubtedly, is much older than that date would suggest.[2]

It is important to keep in mind, however, that such drugs were used in a cultural setting very different from our present society. The use of drugs often had culturally- and religiously-sanctioned goals and involved ceremonial practices. Any use of drugs outside such a context would probably have been considered irresponsible and designed to bring down the wrath of some ancient deity. It is within such an historical framework that we examine the use and abuse of drugs in the Bible.

A note of caution before proceeding, however. While many herbal drugs in the Bible are mentioned by specific name, many others are referred to in a manner making it difficult to equate them with present-day standards. This, coupled with the fact that some herbal drugs are used symbolically to represent a human condition or God's judgment, makes the task a challenging one. Examples of the symbolic use of herbal drugs in Scripture include the use of hemlock as a contrast with the fruits of righteousness (Amos 6:12) and as a symbol of God's judgment (Hosea 10:4). However, even here, the choice is quite appropriate since the bitter, poisonous drug of the hemlock conveyed the intent of the passage.

Biblical Mandate and Herbal Drugs

After God's creation of various kinds of plants and trees on the third day, we are told that: *The Lord God took the man and put him in the garden of Eden to work it and take care of it* (Gen. 2:15NIV).

While we don't normally think of this passage as having any relevance to drugs, it is the case, nevertheless, that it represents God's mandate for man to cultivate the plants of His creation. This would include not only those plants used for food but those containing various chemicals (drugs) of medicinal value as well. It is apparent that man, from the beginning, has played a significant role in the development of herbal drugs.

It also appears that many truly harmful or poisonous plants are the result of God's curse on the earth (Gen. 3:17) and that plants await the day of God's redemption along with the rest of creation (Rom. 8:22). While we tend to focus on God's redemptive plan for mankind, we must keep in mind that He has future plans for all of His creation. It is also likely that man's poor stewardship in caring for God's creation has contributed further to the problem. Man's track record has not been good and the possibility, even the likelihood, of continued neglect cannot be ruled out. It is important to remember that any herbal drug can be harmful if taken in large enough amounts; thus, calling certain drugs harmful and others useful, even in a biblical context, is somewhat arbitrary and misleading.

Use of the Mandrake Plant

The first specific Bible reference to the use of a psychoactive herbal drug is that of the mandrake plant (Mandragora officinarum):

During wheat harvest, Reuben went out into the fields and found some mandrake plants, which he brought to his mother Leah. Rachel said to Leah, "Please give me some of your son's mandrakes." But she said to her, "Wasn't it enough that you took away my husband? Will you take my son's mandrakes too?" "Very well," Rachel said, "he can sleep with you tonight in return for your son's mandrakes." So when Jacob came in from the fields that evening, Leah went out to meet him. "You must sleep with me," she said. "I have hired you with my son's mandrakes." So he slept with her that night (Gen. 30:14-16, NIV).

The mandrake plant, a milder relative of the deadly nightshade, was found in uncultivated fields throughout the eastern Mediterranean of Bible times.[3] The plant contains several powerful psychoactive drugs (atropine, scopolamine, and hyoscyamine) and has a body and fleshy root that, with a little imagination, resemble the human body.[4] Because of its unusual shape, all kinds of properties have been attributed to its nature.

While there were some recognized medical uses of the mandrake plant in biblical times, the present passage appears to emphasize its "love-making" properties. Unfortunately, the mandrake plant has sustained an unwarranted reputation as an aphrodisiac and this passage does nothing to improve its image. In spite of the mandrake plant, Rachael remained barren until God remembered her and opened her womb (Gen. 30:22). She then became pregnant and gave birth to a son, whom she named Joseph. What a marvelous example of God's intervention in a case of misguided reliance on herbal drugs.

Drug Abuse and Sorcery

One of the most interesting but less obvious reference to drugs in the Bible is that associated with occult practices. The sorcerers and other practitioners of the occult used drugs to cast spells on their victims and were, undoubtedly, the closest thing there was to a pharmacist of that period. They probably guarded their secret potions and ceremonial concoctions with great care and recorded many such recipes in occult writings of the time. This seems to be suggested by the passage in Acts 19:18-19, where Paul's converts at Ephesus confessed their evil practice of sorcery and burned their scrolls in public. It is of interest to note that this was done at no small sacrifice to the converts. The scrolls were calculated to be of great monetary worth, which clearly reflects the value placed on such records.

However, the clearest example of the close ties between drugs and sorcery in the Bible is the fact that some translations of the word "sorcery" may actually be equally well translated "drug abuse". In Rev. 9:21, the words "sorceries" (KJV) or "magic arts" (NIV) are translations of the Greek word "pharmakeia",[5] literally meaning "enchantment with drugs". In a similar manner, the words "sorcerers" (KJV) or "those who practice magic arts" (NIV) in Rev. 21:8 and in Rev. 22:15 are translations of the Greek words "pharmakeus" and "pharmakos",[6] respectively, with both words literally meaning "enchanter with drugs".

It would appear, from these texts, that occult practices and drug abuse went hand in hand, and where you found one you undoubtedly found the other. Furthermore, it seems quite appropriate to refer to such occult practices as examples of drug abuse since drugs were used for their mind-altering and perceptual-distorting effects and not for medicinal or other beneficial purposes. From such an ignoble beginning, the Greek word "pharmakos" later referred to herbal drugs used for medicinal purposes and, more recently, serves as a basis for our words, "pharmacists" and "pharmacology"—the study of drugs.[7]

The Bible's position on occult practices is unequivocal and worthy of note in the present context. Such practices are said to be detestable to the Lord (Deut. 18:10-12) and are strongly condemned in both the Old (Lev. 19:26,31; Deut. 18:10-14) and New Testaments (Gal. 5:19-21; Rev. 21:8). Furthermore, they are listed among the acts of the sinful nature in contrast to the fruits of the Spirit (Gal. 5:19-22) as well as being subject to God's final judgment (Rev. 21:8). In light of the close biblical ties between the occult and drug abuse, God's condemnation of the occult, most certainly, would include His condemnation of this form of drug abuse as well. It is important to keep in mind, however, that references to occult practices in the Bible represent only one form of drug abuse.

Biblical Accounts of Alcohol Abuse

Grape vines have been cultivated from very ancient times and have always been a source of great commercial worth as well as social concern. The natural yeast of grapes begins to ferment into wine in a matter of days and it is unlikely that ancient people knew any way to prevent this from occurring. While, in all likelihood, alcohol was discovered following accidental fermentation, its use was commonplace in biblical times and more is said about this form of drug abuse in the Bible than any other form. The earliest reference to alcohol abuse appears to be Noah's drunkenness. Here, we read: *Noah, a man of the soil, proceeded to plant a vineyard. When he drank some of its wine, he became drunk and lay uncovered inside his tent* (Gen. 9:20-21, NIV).

While we are not told how much wine Noah consumed, it was enough to make him drunk and to cause him to be caught in a shameful situation. The reaction of Noah's sons to his nakedness brought down their father's wrath on the generations of one of them and changed the course of human history. While this incident is not what Noah is remembered for, it does indicate the pernicious nature of alcohol abuse, even in the life of a godly man.

Another equally tragic example of over-indulgence was when Lot's desire to enjoy life in Sodom, tragically, resulted in drunken incest (Gen. 19:32-35). The resulting sons became the Moab and Ammon nations which were the enemies of God's people for centuries.

Apparently, the problem of over-indulgence also occurred in the most unexpected contexts as well. In his first letter to the Corinthian church, Paul is highly critical of their practice of the Lord's Supper. Some participants were getting drunk while others were treating the occasion as a substitute for eating and drinking in the home (I Cor. 11:20-22). While one might ask how such a condition could develop, it is simply another example of how pervasive the problem of alcohol abuse can become, even within the Christian church of the first century.

Lest one falsely conclude that examples of alcohol abuse were limited to God's chosen people, we need only to be reminded of King Xerxes' problem with drunkenness (Esther 1:10-20). Historical sources indicate that the Persians drank large quantities of wine and that it was their general practice to make weighty decisions while under its influence.[8] Such seems to be the case with Xerxes' deposal of his disobedient wife as queen while he was in high spirits from wine. While this self-serving act was obviously motivated by his drunken condition and created a potential crisis, God used the occasion to elevate Esther to the position of queen (Esther 2:17).

In a clear and precise manner, the Bible spells out the evils of drunkenness.

- It provokes anger (Prov. 20:1),
- it confuses the mind and
- it distorts one's judgment (Prov. 31:4-5; Isa. 28:7),
- it leads to violence (Prov 4:17),
- it inflames the passions (Isaiah 5:11).

Is it any wonder that tragedy or ungodliness is so often associated with biblical accounts of alcohol abuse? It is also of interest to note that God strongly condemns drunkenness and that it is listed, along with sorcery, as an act of the sinful nature and contrasted with the fruits of the Spirit (Gal. 5:19-21). Scripture further states that those who practice such behavior will not inherit the kingdom of God (I Cor. 6:10).

Other Possible Drugs of Abuse

While the preceding biblical examples of drug abuse are highly specific, other mentions of herbs and their potential for abuse are more speculative. Thus, we must proceed with caution and make sure we do not read into the text more than is intended. With this in mind, mention might be made of the biblical "tares" (KJV) or "weeds" (NIV) referred to in Jesus' parable of the kingdom of heaven (Matt. 13:24-30, 36-43). This weedy grass was probably the bearded darnel[9] (Lolium temulentum) that flourished in the fields of the eastern Mediterranean. The darnel seed is host to an ergot-like fungus which is known to have hallucinogenic properties. While not as powerful as LSD (lysergic-acid-diethylamide), the drug contained in this fungus has similar effects in producing experiences of sensory, emotional and psychological impact.

This being the case, it is hard to believe that the people of Bible times did not discover the powerful effects of this herb, albeit, perhaps, by accident. It is also very likely, although again not specifically stated in the Bible, that this herb may have been one of the most prized possessions of occult practitioners because of its powerful mind-altering effects. It is of further interest to note that the choice of this herb with all of its potential for abuse and harm is used in Jesus' parable as a symbol of the unsaved (Matt. 13:38). This is an interesting choice when you consider the fact that both drug abuse and the rejection of the gospel message have their roots in the same kind of self-centered motivation.

Another example of herbs with abuse potential include biblical references to "gall and wormwood"[10] in Deut. 29:18 and Jer. 9:15 (KJV) and to "gall" in Jer. 8:14 (KJV). While the choice of these particular herbs was intended, primarily, to convey God's judgment on His rebellious chosen people, the potentially dangerous drugs they contain require some practical considerations as well.

Wormwood was the general name given to a group of woody plants (perhaps including gall) with a strong aromatic odor.[11] Absinthe, one of the products made from this group, increases pleasant sensations and fills the mind with pretentious ideas. When used in excess, it may cause stupor and the gradual diminution of intellectual capabilities. Again, it is hard to believe that, in light of the powerful mind-altering effects of these herbs, people of Bible times were not familiar with their use. At the very least, one would expect these herbs to be among those used in occult practices.

It is of interest to note that the NIV translation chooses not to identify these herbs by name but, rather, to stress the underlying spiritual application, God's punishment of sin. Because of the problem of accurately identifying many plants in the Bible, it is difficult to speculate on how many additional herbs might have been abused for one reason or another. The previously mentioned mandrake plant was, undoubtedly, used in the magical practices of the occult, possibly as a charm against evil spirits. It is also highly likely that the Israelites were familiar with the opium poppy and its psychoactive properties as well as with other herbal compounds, probably as a result of their captivity in Egypt. Thus, the opportunity for abusing a wide variety of herbal drugs was clearly available.

Use of Herbal Drugs for Medicinal Purposes

It would be grossly unfair to discuss drugs of the Bible without pointing out that many herbal preparations have great potential for medical use if used properly. This means, of course, that they be used in amounts well below the level of abuse potential and that they are designed to treat a particular malady. In this context, herbal drugs may be consumed or applied topically, whichever addresses the specific treatment need. For all of its bad reputation, the mandrake plant was used for some medicinal purposes, probably for its narcotic and purgative effects.[12]

It is also clear that, in spite of the wide-spread abuse of alcohol in Bible times, the limited medical benefits of the drug were not overlooked. In Paul's advice to Timothy (I Tim. 5:23), he admonishes him to: *Stop drinking only water, and use a little wine because of your stomach and your frequent illnesse*s (NIV). This passage is not an endorsement of drunkenness but a clear recognition of the quieting and settling effects of small amounts of alcohol. The emphasis here is clearly on "little" and, in no way, is a contradiction to what has been previously said about the dangers of alcohol. Drawing the line between the proper and improper uses of alcohol is not an easy task and one can certainly understand why church leaders prefer not to dwell on this particular passage of Scripture. Fortunately, this section of Scripture is rich in spiritual truths and one's attention can be easily diverted to more acceptable admonitions.

Most certainly, the medicinal benefits of the opium poppy were recognized, although the reason for its beneficial effects was not understood. The opium poppy contains the drug morphine which is recognized for its sedative and pain-killing effects. The problem was, as is the case today, that morphine and other similar drugs are highly addictive and one can easily make the transition from use into abuse.

Additional Old Testament examples of the medical use of herbs include the topical application of a lump of figs to treat boils (Isa. 38:21) and the use of certain leaves for medicinal purposes (Ezek. 47:12). Evidently, the Old Testament prophets were not only God's messengers for their time but were also equipped with considerable practical knowledge about the use of herbs.

New Testament examples of the medical use of herbal products include the use of oil and wine by the Samaritan to heal the wounds of the robbery victim (Luke 10:34) and the offer of wine and myrrh to Christ while He was hanging on the cross (Mark 15:23). While Christ refused the offer, both of these occasions indicate a clear recognition of the potential healing and sedative effects of the products. Two herbal products, myrrh and aloe, were also recognized for their preservative properties and were used in preparing Christ's body for burial (John 19:39). Finally, the rue shrub mentioned in Luke 11:42 was a tithable garden plant that had some medicinal value. While it was used primarily as a culinary spice, the oil of its leaves was apparently used to treat a wide variety of medical conditions, including dizziness, epilepsy and inflammation.[13]

From today's perspective, these examples indicate that a fairly sophisticated and extensive knowledge of herbal pharmacology existed in Bible times. While Scripture says nothing specific about the medical practice of Luke, the beloved physician (Col. 4:14, KJV), it is highly probable that such knowledge was readily available to him and was used in his missionary trips with Paul.

Concluding Comments

What, then, can one conclude from our discussion of drugs in the Bible? For one thing, we can certainly discount any view that suggests drug problems are a product of the twentieth century. Although the Bible was written in ancient times and reflects the culture of that period, it is replete with examples of drug-related problems. Israel and the nations that surrounded her made wide use of herbal drugs as an integral part of their diverse social practices. One major difference from the drug scene of today, however, is the fact that drugs abused in Bible times were herbal preparations. In contrast, most of the drugs abused today are synthetic preparations (made in the laboratory) and readily available in tablet or capsule form.

A few herbal drugs (e.g., marijuana) remain as part of the current scene and present unique problems in terms of regulating access and availability. A case in point is the fact that large, home-grown crops of marijuana are periodically uncovered by police and drug officials in Los Angeles and other areas. Since such activity is conducted on private properties, it becomes virtually impossible to detect, let alone regulate, such practices.

Perhaps even more important than demonstrating that drug problems have been around for a long time, is the fact that the Bible makes a clear distinction between the practices of drug use and abuse. Since people of Bible times had the same difficulty that we do today in exercising self restraint, it is important that the Bible recognizes this distinction and makes such examples available for our instruction. This the Bible has done and, in the process, provided us with a most valuable resource for tackling drug problems of today.

God's Word demonstrates the principles of proper drug use as well as flagging those areas of our lives that may lead to drug abuse. The Bible accurately describes man's true nature and his propensity to sin in all areas of life, including those areas related to drug practices. By the same token, God's message of deliverance from sin found in Scripture, gives us great hope of God's power to deliver young people from drug problems today.

Key questions answered by this chapter include:

1. Were there serious drug problems in biblical times?
2. What Old Testament mandate relates to herbal drugs?
3. What is the first psychoactive herbal drug mentioned in the Bible?
4. What evidence is there that biblical sorcery involved drug abuse?
5. What type of drug abuse receives the most biblical attention?

6. What are some biblical examples of the harmful effects of alcohol?
7. What herbal drugs were abused in biblical times?
8. What drugs were used for medicinal purposes in the Bible?
9. Can the Bible serve as a guide for today's drug problems?

Notes

Chapter Four

Drug Abuse and the Christian's Body

Tom was a 30-year-old man living with a woman who had two children from a previous marriage. Since he had also fathered a two-year-old child with her and she was pregnant with her fourth child, they decided to get married and provide some sense of family and stability for the children. While the woman had grown up in a Christian home, her interest in spiritual things had waned since marriage to her first husband.

Although Tom had been brought up as a Catholic, he had never made a profession of faith in Christ. However, during premarital couseling, Tom accepted the Lord and they started their marriage on what appeared to be a high spiritual note—a happy ending, one might say in light of today's standards. However, there was one problem. Tom had a long history of drug abuse and had been in and out of "self-help" and "drug-rehabilitation" programs since high school. The treatment programs had not worked and Tom continued his addiction by joining his buddies on weekends in heavy drinking and drug abuse. He was a good worker and a responsible father and husband during the week, but saw nothing wrong with taking off weekends for a little "macho" fun with his friends. In spite of his wife's protest, he continued such a practice until his untimely death.

After purchasing illegal drugs one Saturday night in a nearby town, Tom returned home around 2:00 AM Sunday morning and began to consume large amounts of beer. The combined effects of the drugs and alcohol along with his borderline diabetes caused a fatal heart attack. Wondering why he had not come to bed upon returning from his drug binge, his wife went downstairs with her oldest son and found Tom dead on the kitchen floor.

The drug addiction was such a powerful driving force in Tom's life that nothing else seemed to matter. Furthermore, Tom was an unlikely candidate for change at his wife's request. In spite of his borderline diabetes, he was a large and muscular man who took pride in his strength and energy. Neither he nor his wife had given much consideration to the possible physical consequences of his drug abuse. As is true with many teenagers and young adults, the physical consequences of such behavior were overlooked because of some sense of physical invulnerability.

In general, all forms of non-medical use of drugs constitute abuse. As Christians, we have a two-fold responsibility:

- to review what the Bible teaches regarding our physical bodies; and
- to demonstrate how drug abuse is totally inconsistent with all of these teachings.

While the message of the Bible addresses, primarily, our spiritual needs, it is surprising to discover how much it says about our physical body. Furthermore, what the Bible says about our body has a clear bearing on how we view drug abuse.

The Human Body: God's Magnificent Creation

Have you ever marveled at the complexity and beauty of the human body—how well proportioned it is and how efficiently it functions? In my thirty plus years in education, I have taught numerous courses which deal with human anatomy and physiology, and I never cease to wonder at this masterpiece we call the body. In my judgment, this is not fortuitous at all, but a clear indication of God's design and purpose.

Let us look at some Scriptural passages that speak about this magnificent creation. First of all, we are told that we are *"made in the image of God"* (Gen. 1:27). Admittedly, this passage refers, primarily, to the non-physical attributes of God's creation since God is a Spirit (John 4:24). However, I find it hard to believe that *"made in the image of God"* doesn't also have some physical implications as well. Why would God express His creative power in such a magnificent way if He were not interested in making a statement? I believe the human body is a clear reflection of God's greatness and a statement of His provisions for our existence while on earth.

Just one example of His bountiful physical provision for us will suffice. Our heart muscle is about the size of an adult fist and is an amazing pumping station. It beats about 70 times a minute and pumps out approximately 75 milliliters of blood with each beat. Since the amount of blood in the adult human body is about 5 liters, the heart completes an entire circulation of our blood approximately every minute.[1] It does this work minute after minute for each day, month and year of our lives. Do you know of anything else that matches the work capacity of this astounding organ? God's physical provision for us is clearly indicated in this instance as is true in so many others that could be mentioned. Indeed, we are *"fearfully and wonderfully made"* (Psa. 139:14).

While this body is subject to decay and death, the Scripture further dignifies it by stressing its literal resurrection upon Christ's return (Phil. 3:21). There is no question but that this speaks of the physical body, since this "lowly" (NIV) or "vile" (KJV) body has its origin from the earth and is the instrument of sin.[2] The good news is that our physically resurrected bodies will be transformed *"like unto His glorious body"* (Phil. 3:21). We get a glimpse of what this body might be like in Christ's Transfiguration upon the Mount (Matt.17:2).

One final comment about God's magnificent creation, the human body. It has always fascinated me that Paul chose the human body as an analogy of the church (I Cor. 12:14-31). Could anything express the desired inter-relatedness and inter-dependency of segments of the church better than the human body? I doubt it seriously. The concreteness of the human body is a splendid visual reminder of what the church should be and the need for unity among its diverse membership.

The Human Body: God's Temple

It is of interest to note that in his letters to the Corinthian church, Paul refers to the physical body as the temple of God (I Cor. 3:16, II Cor. 6:16) or the temple of the Holy Spirit (I Cor. 6:19).

Have you ever wondered why this particular analogy was chosen in writing to the Corinthians? Perhaps, it had something to do with the fact that Corinthian Christians had come out of the pagan religious practices of their wide open and wicked city and were all too familiar with the temple built in honor of Venus[3]—the goddess of love. Apparently, this temple played a key role in the pagan worship of the city and employed a large number of prostitutes to serve the worshipers.

One of the strongest ways to make a point is to do so by pointing out contrasts, and Paul took full advantage of the Corinthians' past and of their environment. As was true for the Corinthians, our body is to be the temple of the true and living God, and our lives are to stand in strong contrast with the pagan practices of the surrounding world. This sense of contrast is highlighted by Paul's words in II Cor. 6:16-17: *"What agreement is there between the temple of God and idols? For we are the temple of the living God. . . . Therefore come out from them and be separate, says the Lord"* (NIV).

Quite apart from the strong point Paul communicates to the Corinthian Church, what does it mean for our physical body to be the temple of God? A number of things immediately come to mind —a sacred and holy place, a place of worship, and a place of residence.

God's Holy Spirit desires to take up residence in our body but will do so only to the degree that we are willing to yield to His will. God will not reside where He is not welcome. We must desire to make our bodies a sacred and holy place of worship and, by so doing, become a fitting place for God's Holy Spirit to dwell.

Of course, we cannot do this in our own strength but, along with Paul, are confident that He who started the good work in our life will bring it to completion (Phil. 1:6).

The idea that God's Holy Spirit dwells in the body of the believer is such an astounding one that it is difficult for us to grasp its full meaning and implication for our lives. While this may be true, two things appear to be very clear, however. First of all, the dwelling of God's Holy Spirit in our bodies is made possible only because of the great cost paid by Christ. We are reminded in I Cor. 6:20 that we are to glorify God in our bodies because we are bought with a price. The implication here is very clear—without such a price having been paid, glorifying God through the presence of His Holy Spirit in our bodies would be impossible.

Secondly, God's Holy Spirit dwelling in our bodies is a confirmation of God's covenant with the believer and a statement of His desire to fellowship with them. After reminding the believers that they are His temple, God promises: *"I will live with them and walk among them, and I will be their God, and they will be my people"* (II Cor. 6:16, NIV). What a tremendous comfort and assurance for the child of God.

While the dwelling of God's Holy Spirit in our bodies is a blessing beyond description, a word of warning accompanies this experience. We are warned that God will destroy him who destroys God's temple—the body (I Cor. 3:17). We find strong language here and it should put believers on guard as to how they view and treat their bodies. If Christians had a renewed vision of their bodies as a temple of God, I'm convinced it would drastically change their attitudes and practices regarding many things, including those related to drug abuse.

Healthy Bodies as a Christian Testimony

The prevailing view in the scientific community and among the news media is that religion has a negative effect on physical health. While such a conclusion is based upon little or no data and research on the relationship of religion and health has been strongly biased by anti-religious beliefs, the myth that religion makes us ill lives on.[4] Are Christians, in fact, less healthy than non-Christians? Is it possible that they are, at least, as healthy as non-Christians or, maybe, even healthier?

A recent report addresses this issue. Research conducted by one of the nation's leading religion-health scientists, who just happens to also be a Christian, indicates a very positive influence of religious beliefs on health.[5] People who go to church have clinically-significant lower blood pressure than people who do not, and religious commitment reduces the potential of physical stress. Furthermore, these findings are still highly significant after they had been adjusted for such factors as weight, smoking habits, and age.[6]

What do you suppose accounts for such positive findings? While a complete explanation may not be possible, a strong commitment to religious beliefs, undoubtedly, reduces various types of risk-taking behavior such as smoking and heavy drinking.[7] Such a strong commitment may also promote healthy practices like relaxation, exercise, and prayer as a form of meditation.[8] Apparently, religious people tend to cultivate habits that show respect for their bodies. It would appear that a healthy body can be an effective Christian witness by testifying to the commitment one has in taking care of God's temple.

While the Old Testament passages that command us not to dishonor our body (Lev. 19:28; 21:5, Deut. 14:1) were given specifically to the children of Israel and designed to distinguish them from the pagan practices of the surrounding nations, they have equal applicability to our Christian lives today.

The value of physical exercise to our health is clearly recognized by both Christians and non-Christians; however, the Bible puts such exercise in its proper perspective relative to spiritual exercise (I Tim. 4:8). Unfortunately, the KJV of this passage which reads *"for bodily exercise profiteth little"* does not convey the full meaning of the text. Rather than meaning bodily exercise doesn't have much value, the passage really means it has value for a little time, namely the temporal period of our existence here on earth.[9] A more accurate translation of the passage is found in the NIV which reads, *"...physical training is of some value"*. However, in contrast to the temporal benefits of physical exercise to our bodies, godliness has value both in this life and the life to come (I Tim. 4:8).

One final observation about healthy bodies and the believer. While here on earth, Christ physically healed people primarily to confirm His power over sin as is clearly pointed out in the healing of the paralytic (Mark 2:10-11; Luke 5:24). However, Christ was also a true servant of humanity and healed out of compassion and concern for the physical welfare of people. Thus, Christ's healing of sickness and disease put the seal of approval on our reverence for the physical body and our desire to present it as a testimony to God's grace.

After all that has been said about the relationship of healthy bodies and Christian testimonies, we must not make the serious mistake of equating physical health with a certain degree of spirituality. From all of the information we have, there is no reason to believe that Paul was an outstanding physical specimen and yet his life was one of great spiritual depth. His *"thorn in the flesh"*, whatever it was, became an effective testimony of God's grace working in his life (II Cor. 12:7). In the same manner, believers who are physically handicapped or experiencing failing health for one reason or another can also be an effective testimony of God's grace in their life.

Drug Abuse and God's Temple

Now that we have examined what the Bible has to say about the human body, we want to examine evidence which demonstrates how incompatible drug abuse is with these biblical teachings. While the actual pattern of abuse may vary considerably according to the particular drug taken, one common characteristic appears to emerge. The lifestyle of the abuser is mainly oriented around obtaining and taking the drug.[10]

While one might argue that all forms of non-medical use of drugs do not reflect such a lifestyle, any use of drugs not medically supervised runs the risk of becoming so intensified as to qualify. With this being the case, the distinction between non-medical use and abuse of drugs becomes arbitrary and of little practical value.

Let us now look at two specific ways in which drug abuse adversely affects the body and thus violates biblical teaching. First of all, drug abuse brings the physical body under captivity. The basic question raised here is, "Who or what rules over our body?" Do drugs rule our body with their ever-present demands for satisfaction or does God rule our body through the presence of His Holy Spirit? Both cannot rule as is clearly indicated in Eph. 5:18 where we read: *"And be not drunk with wine, wherein is excess; but be filled with the Spirit"* (KJV).

The clearest example of drugs ruling over our body is seen in the case of physical dependence. When a person takes a drug repeatedly for an extended period of time, the body undergoes physical changes that eventually trick the body into believing that the "drug state" is the normal condition. Of course, the individual must continue to take the drug to maintain this "drug state" since failure to do so will produce some form of withdrawal symptoms. In general, the degree of withdrawal symptoms reflects the degree to which the body has been captive to the drug.

While it is commonly assumed that illicit (illegal) drugs have the greatest potential for bringing the body under captivity, this is not necessarily the case. Alcohol, a readily available and legal drug, is often associated with withdrawal symptoms that are more severe and potentially dangerous than those associated with illicit drugs.

A related issue to that of physical dependence is the adulterants which often accompany illicit drug use.[11] In street-level drug trafficking, adulterants (also called fillers) are added to the drug, usually to dilute them. While in some instances drugs may be diluted by a simple sugar powder, in other instances adulterants are unknown and stand the chance of being highly toxic as was true in the case of Billy.

While living in the dormitory at a Christian college, Billy experienced considerable difficulty in concentrating on his studies. Unknown to Billy, his roommate had been taking "speed" (a form of amphetamine) to help him concentrate and to keep him awake while studying for exams. When Billy told his roommate of his difficulty, his roommate convinced him to try a little speed before his upcoming midterm exams. Billy felt guilty about doing it and knew that his parents would be upset if they found out; however, he decided to try it. Unfortunately, trying it proved to be very helpful and "speed" became his formula for school success.

While Billy was not sure where the speed came from, he thought his roommate's source was some contact at the local mall. On the last occasion when Billy received the drug from his roommate, he began to hallucinate and became violently ill. When the reaction did not quickly pass, his roommate, in fear of exposure and concern for Billy's welfare, rushed him to the emergency room of the local hospital. After keeping him overnight for observation, Billy felt better and he was released from the hospital. It was later discovered that Billy had taken a dose of DOM (an amphetamine derivative which produces hallucinogenic effects) mixed with a contaminated powder substance rather than his usual speed mixture. As is true with all street drugs, Billy had no way of knowing or checking what he was getting from his roommate.

It is also important to recognize that during the period of its drug captivity, the body pays a heavy biological price. The chronic abuse of some drugs has the potential for impairing cardiovascular functions and increasing the likelihood of certain kinds of cancer.[12] Risk factors of these types appear to be associated with the use of such drugs as alcohol and tobacco. Other types of disease or damage to organs may also occur with drug abuse as is clearly evidenced by liver cirrhosis induced by excessive alcohol consumption.[13] Permitting the body to be brought under any form of captivity by drugs is in specific violation of biblical teachings and a clear example of the desecration of God's temple. God would not be pleased to reside in a dwelling where drugs set the agenda and made the decisions.

In addition to bringing the body under captivity, drug abuse has the potential for an even greater disaster—that of destroying the body. The clearest example of such a potential is seen with the acute (short-term) toxic effects of overdosing on a drug. Sufficiently large doses of any drug can be life-threatening regardless of whether the overdosing is accidental or an attempt to end one's life. Since it is impossible to monitor the quality of street drugs, the abuser loses control over the consequences of his behavior and puts his life in great danger. This is particularly true when street drugs and alcohol are mixed as was the case with Tom (mentioned at beginning of chapter). You'll recall that Tom's heavy drinking of beer after an evening of abusing street drugs with his friends proved to be fatal.

While overdosing is the most obvious example of how drug abuse can destroy the body, other examples are equally vivid reminders of the danger of such behavior. For example, the cardiovascular impairment produced by chronic (long-term) drug abuse can result in heart disease and death. In the same manner, lung cancer resulting from chronic tobacco abuse, or liver cirrohosis resulting from excessive alcohol use can also eventually result in death. The difference between these effects and those resulting from acute overdosing is simply a matter of time—whether they occur gradually or suddenly.

While the above examples clearly demonstrate the specific link between drug abuse and destruction of the body, other potentially destructive factors may be related to peripheral, risk-taking behavior indulged in by the abuser. One such example is the sharing of needles with other drug abusers and the great potential for transmitting disease and infection by such a practice. Some forms of hepatitis (inflammation of the liver) are transmitted by dirty needles shared among drug abusers.

While such an effect is serious enough, perhaps the greatest life-threatening danger associated with sharing needles is the potential for transmitting the AIDS (acquired immune deficiency syndrome) virus. Unlike many viruses transmitted by casual contact, the AIDS virus can be transmitted only if it enters the blood of the recipient. The sharing of needles by abusers produces a strong possibility that, if AIDS infected blood is on the needle, the next person using it will become infected. Since no known cure is presently available for AIDS,[14] the prognosis for those infected with the virus is bleak indeed. While the drug abuser may not focus on such peripheral, risk-taking behavior as needle sharing, it could prove to be the most destructive of all forms of behavior.

As was the case with bringing the body under captivity, the destruction of the body by drug abuse is in specific violation of biblical teachings regarding the sanctity of our body. To destroy the body is to destroy God's temple and this carries with it the promise that God will destroy the person who indulges in such behavior (I Cor. 3:17). Such a judgment should be enough to discourage any thinking Christian from becoming involved in the non-medical use of drugs.

Drug Abuse and God's Purpose for Our Body

After reviewing the destructive power of drug abuse, we must ask ourselves the most basic of all questions. How does drug abuse fit in with God's purpose and plan for the Christian's body? Scripture indicates that we are to honor God with our body (I Cor. 6:20) and we are to offer our bodies as living sacrifices to God (Rom. 12:1). Stated in the simplest of terms, God's purpose for our bodies is that we live for Him and not for ourselves. How we treat our physical bodies should not serve our own desires but, rather, reflect a spiritual act of worship (Rom. 12:1).

We need, in particular, to impress this idea on the minds of our young people. Since their physical desires are so strong, they may feel that presenting their bodies as an act of worship is an unattainable goal; if not unattainable, then certainly something rarely experienced. They, like we, must recognize the basic nature of sin in their lives. Sin distracts us from the task at hand—that of honoring God with our bodies. By the same token, anything that distracts us from this task is, by nature, sin.

Having come full circle in our discussion, we must finally recognize drug abuse for what it really is—sin.[15] Are we overly simplifying the drug problem with such a ceremonial response? I don't believe that's the case. We must recognize that the root of such destructive behavior toward our bodies is our sin nature. Recognizing drug abuse as sin not only indicates why it is totally unacceptable behavior for the Christian (young or old) but also explains why it is so destructive to God's purpose for our bodies. Sin and God's Holy Spirit cannot simultaneously rule in our bodies.

Like any sin, drug abuse must be confessed for what it is, and one has the promise of God's forgiveness (I John 1:9). The promise of forgiveness, however, is not to be viewed as a guarantee of immediate deliverance from such behavior (see Chapter 9). Christian workers, parents and young people in particular need to see drug abuse as sin and not be bamboozled by the attempts of the secular world to excuse such behavior, or explain it away in non-spiritual terms.

Key questions answered by this chapter include:

1. How does the human body reflect God's magnificent creation?

2. What does it mean for the human body to be God's temple?

3. Can a healthy body be a Christian testimony?

4. How does drug abuse bring our bodies under captivity?

5. How does drug abuse destroy our bodies?

6. Does God's plan for our bodies leave any room for drug abuse?

7. Is it sinful to abuse our bodies with drugs?

Notes

Chapter Five

Drug Abuse and the Christian's Mind

Sue was the only child of parents who can best be described as nominal Christians. While they attended a liberal Protestant church, their professed faith appeared to have little impact on their family life or associations outside the home. When Sue was a freshman in high school, her father died as the result of a tragic work-related accident. Although her mother received a large financial settlement from her husband's company which enabled them to live comfortably, they both expressed anger that God would let such a thing happen to them.

Over time, the mother retired more and more from the social scene and her major goal in life became that of living through her daughter. The mother truly loved Sue and spent a lot of time with her. However, she pushed Sue to the limit in everything she did as a means of compensating for her loss and fulfilling vicariously her own girlhood dreams. She insisted that Sue excel academically as well as strive to be the best in her extra-curricular activities. Although Sue frequently complained about the pressure she felt, her mother always responded by saying, "You'll get nowhere by being a quitter." Sue complied out of fear of being rejected by her mother.

Sue was a beautiful girl and soon learned that by being flirtatious she could get the attention of any high school boy she wanted. The flirting soon led to sexual promiscuity and experimentation with drugs. By her sophomore year, Sue was drinking heavily and addicted to marijuana. On occasion, she also used cocaine. Sue soon realized that drugs covered up her guilt about being loose with boys and not meeting the expectations of her mother as well as providing an exciting experience of freedom.

When under the influence of drugs nothing seemed to matter and all was well in her little world. The mind-altering effect of drugs was her escape from the world of reality and she reveled in it. Fortunately, this is not the end of the story for Sue. She was eventually able to replace these feelings with her own set of values (free of her mother's demands) and started making good, healthy decisions on her own.

The popular advertisement on television depicting "your brain on drugs" being like "an egg in a frying pan" may not be a very accurate description of what drugs do to the brain, but it certainly is an attention getter. As one author suggests,[1] your brain on drugs may, actually, be more like "throwing it in the refrigerator" since some drugs (e.g., cocaine) appear to cool activity in the brain instead of "heating it up." Regardless of whether drugs "fry" or "freeze" activity in the brain, it is quite obvious that experiences like Sue's indicate psychoactive drugs have a profound effect on mental functions.

Some hallucinogens (e.g., LSD and peyote) are capable of altering perceptions to the degree that a person's "real world" of experience is replaced by a "fantasy world."[2] In such an instance, the person loses all contact with reality. As their name implies, hallucinogens also have the tendency to produce hallucinations and can induce states of consciousness bordering on the psychotic. Is it any wonder that such drugs are sometimes referred to as "phantasticants" (a variation of the word fantastic)? While not all psychoactive drugs produce such profound effects as the hallucinogens, all such drugs result in some degree of distortion or disorganization of a person's mental capacity and ability to recognize reality.

As if these effects were not enough, psychoactive drugs are also known, in some instances, to produce prolonged or irreversible structural damage to brain tissue. The clearest example of this is found with Korsakoff's syndrome, a type of brain damage frequently seen in chronic alcoholics.[3] Such individuals may go for weeks at a time eating very little and consuming large amounts of alcoholic beverages. Since this person is not getting the vitamin (thiamine) needed to carry on metabolic activity, there is a shrinkage or loss of neurons throughout the brain. Such individuals suffer severe memory loses and are greatly impaired in all of their cognitive abilities.

Structural damage, while not yet proven, is also a possibility with LSD. One of the most frightening adverse reactions to LSD is the flashback—the recurrence of symptoms weeks or even months after the drug has been taken. Such experiences may be the result of permanent changes or damage to the brain. Apparently, people using LSD, or even other hallucinogens, may pay both an immediate and long-lasting price for the experience. Fortunately, the mind-altering effects of psychoactive drugs are more common than structural damage resulting from their use.

This chapter addresses these concerns in relationship to what the Bible says about the mind of the Christian. In the context of the present concerns, one might ask why the "mind" has been separated out for special consideration. Isn't the mind merely an expression of how the brain works and, thus, part of the physical body?[4] Shouldn't it simply have been considered as a topic in the preceding Chapter on "Drug Abuse and the Christian's Body"?

While both of these questions could be answered in the affirmative, the effect of psychoactive drugs on the Christian's mind is given special consideration for one very important reason. The mind exercises a powerful controlling influence over the entire body and anything that alters mental faculties also affects the ability of the mind to exercise such control. Since psychoactive drugs alter mental faculties, they also markedly interfere with the mind's ability to bring the body under the control of God's teachings and will for our lives.

The Christian's struggle of the mind over the body is vividly pointed out by Paul in Rom. 7:25 where we read: *"So then with the mind I myself serve the law of God; but with the flesh the law of sin"* (KJV). The Christian's struggle is difficult enough without the picture being further complicated by the destructive effects of psychoactive drugs on our mental faculties. As will be made clear in the following section, God expects more, not less, from the minds of Christians.

God's Plan for the Christian Mind

The Bible has a great deal to say about the Christian's mind and how it should operate. In every instance, God's plan for our mind challenges us to raise our level of awareness and commitment far above that of the non-believer and even above that of our own expectations.

One of the key elements in God's plan is that **we come to Him with a willing mind** and that He, in return will accept us the way we are (II Cor. 8:12). Coming to God with a willing mind clearly implies a voluntary submission to His will and law. Such an attitude is not only critical at the time we appropriate God's plan of salvation to our personal life but equally important at all subsequent stages of our growth and maturity in Christ. It is also a comforting thought to know that we are accepted on the basis of our willingness to come rather than on the basis of our abilities or assets. Many of us would have difficulty approaching God if it were any other way. The Christian experience is an equal-opportunities endeavor and not the exclusive right of the rich, the famous, or even of the poor.

A second key element in God's plan is that **we love God with all our heart, soul and mind** (Matt. 22:37; Mark 12:30). It is quite possible that the words "heart, soul and mind" in this passage refer to the same thing (all our power) or simply to different aspects of mental functions (will, affection and understanding).[5] Such an interpretation would appear to be consistent with the passage in Prov. 23:7 which talks about man *"thinking in his heart"* (KJV). To love God with all of our mind is something all of us should aspire to as Christians but, obviously, have not yet mastered in our present state. It might even be more appropriate to suggest that a "mind to love God" with such intensity requires a commitment that few of us are prepared to make.

It is also of interest to note that Scripture gives us a yardstick of our love for God—our love of our brother. In I John 4:20, we are reminded that: *"If a man say, I love God, and hateth his brother, he is a liar: for he that loveth not his brother whom he hath seen, how can he love God whom he hath not seen?"* (KJV) It appears that our mental commitment to love should be directed outward as well as upward and that the two expressions are inextricably related.

Perhaps the most fascinating element of all in God's plan is found in Phil. 2:5, where we are told to, *"Let this mind be in you, which was also in Christ Jesus"* (KJV). What a mind-boggling thought to contemplate what it means to have the mind and attitudes of Christ. We are told that the Lord's thoughts are higher than our thoughts (Isa. 55:9), and it seems almost disrespectful to suggest that we could share the thoughts of our Savior. However, this passage, again, reflects a direction or pattern for our lives which requires a clear mental commitment on our part. This direction or pattern for our lives would appear to include at least two critical characteristics.

First, we are **to imitate the self-humbling attitude of Christ** so clearly outlined for us in Phil. 2:6-8. Here we read: *"Who, being in very nature God, did not consider equality with God something to be grasped, but made himself nothing, taking the very nature of a servant, being made in human likeness. And being found in appearance as a man, he humbled himself and became obedient to death—even death on a cross*" (NIV). How contrary such a mental set is to our human nature and, yet, what lofty goals God sets for the Christian's mind.

The second direction or pattern expressed in *"having the mind of Christ"* would be **to yield our minds to God's will for our lives.** Christ indicated that *"...my meat is to do the will of Him that sent me..."* (John 4:34, KJV). To *"have the mind of Christ,"* we, too, must commit our mind to do God's will. His perfect will is clearly laid out for us in the person, life and teaching of His Son. Not only is God's plan for the Christian's mind clearly outlined for us in Scripture, it is also sharply contrasted with the mindset of the unbeliever. We are told in Rom. 8:7 that the sinful mind is hostile toward God and cannot submit to His will. Many times we lose sight of the fact that our mindset should be different than that of the unbeliever and, thus, miss out on God's blessing for our lives.

What will be our response to God's plan for the Christian's mind? Are we up to the challenge or is it something so far beyond our reach that it looms over our heads as an impossible dream? I trust that the former is true and not the latter. However, one thing is crystal clear—such a challenge can only be met with minds that are able to think clearly and whose faculties are unimpeded by the adverse effects of psychoactive drugs. Sound choices accompanied by strong commitment must characterize the activity of our minds and the effects of psychoactive drugs run counter to such activity.

Drug Abuse and the Christian Will

When we use the word "will" a number of mental characteristics come to mind—desire, choice, determination and volition. While these characteristics overlap considerably, perhaps the most important common denominator is the mental power of choice. Once unleashed, this power has tremendous ramifications and is difficult to recapture. As Christians, our mental power of choice should be subject to the will of God. Unfortunately, one cannot make godly choices while being "bombed out" on drugs. Making godly, or even "sound" choices requires a sense of reality in one's interaction with the environment and drug abuse deprives one of that sense. A person may make choices while experiencing hallucinations or some other altered state of consciousness, but you can be sure that the choices are the wrong ones with potentially tragic outcomes.

One clear example of the wrong choice made under such conditions is the story of Jack. Jack was a fun-loving high schooler who was liked by everybody and active in the youth group at his church. His parents knew that Jack drank occasionally, but thought it was relatively harmless. After all, they, too, were social drinkers and frequently entertained other adults in their home while sharing a glass or two of wine. However, on the night of his graduation from high school, Jack went to a party and got drunk. Convincing himself and several of his friends that he could drive them home from the party, he started out. While speeding down the highway, he lost control of his car and hit an on-coming car head on. Two of the friends in his car were killed and one seriously injured. Jack had only minor injuries, due largely to the fact that he was thrown clear of the accident and landed on the soft shoulder of the roadside. The one individual in the on-coming car was also injured, but survived. Jack's decision to drive under the influence of alcohol and to speed in the process was obviously a poor decision. While Jack admitted later that he did not have the state of mind to realize what he was doing on that occasion, the pain and guilt is a burden he will bear the rest of his life.

You may say that this example is far-fetched and unlikely to happen in your family. While that may be the case, I would still caution Christian parents not to get too smug regarding this problem. As was previously indicated, no church or Christian community remains untouched by the drug crisis in our society.[6] Apparently, there are sufficient numbers of young Christians making wrong choices under the influence of alcohol and other drugs to warrant our concern.

The ability of Christians to make godly choices has been and will continue to be critical throughout our spiritual journey. When we accepted Christ as our personal Savior, we did so with a clear understanding of His sacrificial death and our need for forgiveness of sin. The impact of drugs on our thought processes would not have permitted such a decision to be made. As Morey aptly points out in his book, God never saved anyone through chemicals.[7] In the same manner, our daily Christian walk requires that we continue to make godly choices each day. Drugs should not be allowed to cloud our decisions or impede our progress in maturing as Christians. Thus, Morey's statement might be expanded to also say that Christians will never mature spiritually through chemicals, either.

Drug Abuse and Christian Motivation

While the word "motivation" is difficult to define, it essentially attempts to explain why we behave the way we do. Motivation not only implies energy and a driving power, but the channeling of such drive in a particular direction in order to serve some purpose. Unharnessed energy is not motivation; however, when that energy directs one to accomplish a certain objective or attain a certain goal, then it becomes motivation. It is also quite obvious that motivation is, as is also true with choice, a mental process. Unless we are talking about basic animal drives, motivation requires making clear decisions and commitments to certain goals and objectives in our Christian life.

What, then, should be the Christian's motivation? Should we be captive to the same driving forces and objectives as the non-believer? Hopefully not, for the Bible sets a clear pattern for Christian motivation. The overriding characteristic of our motivation should be our love for God. While this is such a simple statement, its application to our lives and the lives of our young people is much more profound.

To say that "our love for God" should characterize our motivation means that such love becomes the primary goal and objective of our lives. Undoubtedly, such a focus is easier said than done. Not only does it imply a personal relationship with Christ, but a constant yielding of our mind to the ministry of the Holy Spirit in order that we might mature in our faith. We are told in Scripture that the Holy Spirit is our teacher and brings to our remembrance the teachings of Christ (John 14:26). Fully yielding our minds to the ministry of God's Holy Spirit is, undoubtedly, the fullest expression of what it means to love God. Again, our young people need to be reminded of this fact.

One might appropriately ask, "What is the driving force that underlies such an expression of love?" The answer resounds from the pages of God's Word, *"We love Him, because He first loved us"* (I John 4:19, KJV). The full expression of His love for us is demonstrated in the gift of His Son as an atoning sacrifice for our sins (I John 4:10). I don't know about you, but I have a great deal of difficulty comprehending the depth of such love. If, with thankful hearts, we make the effort to meditate on such love, we cannot help but be compelled to yield our minds to God's will.

After all that has been said about the nature of Christian motivation, what relevance does it have to our interest in drug abuse? Its relevance is this: drug abuse can adversely affect motivation or it can become a tremendously powerful motivational goal in its own right. In either case, the purpose of God in the lives of our young people is defeated.

The way in which drugs can adversely affect motivation is demonstrated in the life of John. John was a hard-working, straight "A" student until his junior year in high school. He worked on weekends to earn enough money to pay for his first car. He went to church on Sunday with his parents and occasionally worked with the boys and girls in the nearby children's hospital. Suddenly, he started to change; instead of going to his job and the hospital, he spent long hours in his room listening to rap music. He started to hang out with a crowd that was always getting into trouble at school. He had an increasingly hard time remembering what he had learned in school and lost all interest in keeping up his grades. Finally, his parents confronted him, and he admitted that he had been smoking marijuana on a daily basis. He agreed to get help and was eventually able to kick the habit. Once he got back on track, he looked on his past experience with shame and regret.

Considering the long action of marijuana in the body (a long half-life), it is likely that John was under the influence of the drug chronically while using it. Such an effect would certainly explain his general lack of interest and poor motivation.

Drug abuse can also be a motivational goal in itself by consuming the life of the abuser. His or her entire mental set focuses on either the consumption of drugs or unscrupulous ways of obtaining them. The mind of the abuser is obsessed with experiencing a "high" or "trip" and, as a result, he or she has little time for anything else including the things of God. While I don't want to imply that Satan uses drug abuse as his only, or even his primary, way of attacking the minds of young Christians, it most certainly serves his purposes very effectively.

Drug abuse is so consuming of one's mental faculties that there is little room for interest in or focus on the things of God. We are told in James 1:8 that *"... a double minded man is unstable in all his ways"* (KJV). While this passage is describing the doubter, I believe it is equally descriptive of the mind in general conflict—even conflict between drug abuse and godly living. As Morey[8] points out in his book, one cannot love, obey, or worship God in a drug-induced state. Pure (godly) motivation requires that we have total control over our mental faculties, and drug abuse robs us of such control. The message is clear; drug abuse, in any form, has no place in the life of a Christian (young or old) who desires to be filled with godly motivation.

Drug Abuse and the Transforming of the Mind

In light of the possibility of confusing the transforming effects on the mind produced by psychoactive drugs with spiritual transformation spoken of in Scripture, a word of caution is in order, particularly to young people. In Rom. 12:2, we are told: *"And be not conformed to this world: but be ye transformed by the renewing of your mind, that ye may prove what is that good, and acceptable, and perfect, will of God"* (KJV).

The transformation and renewal of mind spoken of in this passage is God-derived, not drug-derived. This is made very clear in the preceding verse (Rom. 12:1), where we are admonished to present our bodies as living sacrifices to God. Such transformation is brought about by the ministry of the Holy Spirit in our lives and has nothing to do with hallucinations or any other drug-induced, altered state of consciousness.

At this juncture, you probably respond by saying, "Isn't such a point obvious?" I would like to think so, but, unfortunately, it is a point that needs to be repeatedly reinforced for one obvious reason. Many young Christians tend to wrongfully equate "feelings" and "sensations" with the reality of their spiritual temperature. If they have a "mountain-top experience" or a "psychological high," then everything must be spiritually attuned. If, on the other hand, such experiences are absent, then something must be drastically lacking in their spiritual lives. Such a contrast can be a major dilemma in the lives of young Christians, since they may be more inclined to equate the genuineness of experience with the intensity of emotions. However, they must be cautious in doing so and remember that God's yardstick for spiritual health has nothing to do with such human judgments.

It is of interest to note that, in at least one instance, the distinction between drug-induced transformation of the mind and spiritual worship has been lost. For example, the Native American (Indian) Church uses the hallucinogen peyote as a sacrament in its religious ceremonies.[9] This church is recognized as a valid church by government authorities and its members may legally possess and use peyote buttons (top of the cactus plant) for such practices. Undoubtedly the members experience some marked changes in their state of consciousness as a result of the effects of peyote.

Does such a practice facilitate "true" worship? Definitely not, not according to biblical standards! The religious practices of the Native American Church constitute an unholy marriage of traditional Christian values with ancient animistic practices of the people. Drugs that alter one's perception of the world and of him- or herself fit right into animistic views.[10]

If peyote contains a spirit (as is assumed in animism), then the plant may speak to the consumer and provide him with special powers of insight. While the members may be gaining powers of insight, those powers, obviously, do not have their source in God.

This is not the type of transforming and renewing of the mind spoken of in Scripture. Let us be warned by such an example not to confuse the power of drugs over our mind with the working of God's Spirit in our lives. This might very well have been the tone of Paul's warning to the Corinthians, where some participants were getting drunk at the Lord's supper (I Cor. 11:20-22).

Concluding Comments

As Christians, we are told in I Peter 1:13, to: *"Prepare your minds for action; be self-controlled"* (NIV). To prepare our minds for action requires that we think clearly and make the right choices; to be self-controlled implies that we are in full charge of our mental faculties and are motivated by our love for God. We cannot meet such a challenge with minds altered by the psychoactive effects of drugs.

Drugs compete with God's plan for control over our minds and thwart any attempt by the Holy Spirit to minister to us. The mind of a Christian young person, in particular, is a spiritual battleground with many competing forces (including drug abuse) jockeying for control. Let us keep our focus on God and not let other factors distract us from maintaining this focus. Our prayer should be for God to give us the strength to do this.

Finally, we need to pass on a word of challenge to young Christians. Decide today, who or what is going to control your mind. God wants your mind in order that you might learn to do His will and experience the fullness of life. Let His love motivate you to live a holy life and serve Him to the best of your ability. Drug abuse, in any form or to any degree, simply won't let that happen.

Key questions answered by this chapter include:

1. Can drugs produce a fantasy world of perception?

2. What is God's plan for the Christian mind?

3. Do psychoactive drugs make it difficult to think clearly?

4. How does drug abuse affect the Christian will?

5. How does drug abuse affect Christian motivation?

6. What is meant by a biblical transforming of the mind?

7. Can the abuse of drugs also transform our mind?

Notes

Chapter Six

Faith, Drugs and Healing

Phil was a 19-year-old male who was receiving in-patient treatment for his cocaine dependency. He was also referred for a psychiatric evaluation because of his severe depression symptoms. He had been freebasing cocaine for two to three months prior to admission to the treatment program five days earlier. Now he was feeling severely depressed and experiencing cocaine cravings. Phil had no history of depression and no family history of psychiatric disorder. However, during childhood he experienced hyperactivity and had a mild learning disability.

At the insistence of school authorities, Phil was prescribed the stimulant Ritalin to help him control his behavior in the classroom. He noted that since that time he had preferred stimulant drugs because they calmed him down. He had received in-patient treatment for cocaine dependency once previously and he'd had two years of complete abstinence before returning on this occasion.

Having been raised in a Christian home, Phil felt a spiritual high during his clean times, although he continued to be somewhat hyper. His parents had repeatedly told him that God could and would deliver him from his dependency if he would only fully trust Him. When returning to cocaine use, Phil lost all spiritual hope and felt abandoned by God. The present depression Phil was experiencing during treatment was due to withdrawal effects from cocaine and did little to alleviate his sense of spiritual failure. Fortunately, in-patient treatment combined with anti-depressant medication got Phil started back on track, although his spiritual confidence continued to suffer for years to come.

Phil's story is an example of the complicated inter-relationship of faith, healing (physical or mental) and drug problems that Christians can encounter in our present society. Many Christians experience a strong resistance to any natural means of healing or treatment, including those that use drugs. Apparently, they feel that turning to natural means of healing represents a weak faith in God. After all, God heals and if they had sufficient faith, wouldn't God take care of the problem without the need to call upon human resources? Unfortunately, this attitude not only includes medical treatment for physical disorders, but psychological treatment for emotional and mental disorders as well.[1] The bottom line of such attitudes is that, if we were right with God, our physical and psychological needs would be met.

In one of his books, Unger[2] shares an example of such an unbalanced view of divine healing and the consequences that ensued. A Christian woman had been miraculously healed by prayer and faith and, as a result, became fanatically opposed to doctors and medicine. Her belief in faith over natural means of healing was so strong that she persuaded her church board to deny membership to medical doctors. While not many Christians would go that far, there is still a tinge of sympathy in the attitudes of some Christians for such a view. Again, this is due to the fact that we tend to measure the depth and genuineness of our faith by what God does in our time of need. After all, we are reminded by Scripture that, if we had the faith of a grain of mustard seed, we would be able to remove mountains (Matt. 17:20). Shouldn't such faith be sufficient for our physical and psychological needs as well?

The critical issue in faith healing is not whether God can heal physically or psychologically. He most certainly can! The question is whether He **chooses** to do so. Sometimes, He does, but not always. Herein lies the basis for a more balanced view of the role of faith healing and medicine. God may miraculously heal someone as a result of faith and prayer; however, He may also choose to heal someone through the use of drugs and other medications as well. In the latter case, the physician (whether he recognizes it or not) is God's instrument of healing. In those instances where the physician is a Christian, this view might be an easy "pill to swallow". Well, the pill is still good medicine even in those instances where the physician is not a Christian. The Bible is replete with examples of God's using ungodly men and nations to fulfill His purpose. So it is with healing.

The purpose of this chapter is two fold:

- to discuss the biblical basis of faith healing and its contemporary characterization; and
- to present the use of drugs under medical supervision as a viable, God ordained alternative to faith healing.

The intent is not to present a negative picture of faith healing but, rather, to demonstrate that drugs can be used in a positive manner to fulfill God's purpose for our lives. In the two previous chapters, we have looked at drugs only in terms of the damage they can cause to our bodies and minds, but we can also demonstrate the rightful place of drugs in the healing professions.

Faith and Biblical Healing

There is a rich tradition of the relationship between faith and healing presented to us in the pages of Scripture. This tradition was established by Christ in His ministry and passed on to the apostles as they carried out the great commission. We are told in Matt. 4:23: *"And Jesus went about all Galilee...healing all manner of sickness and all manner of disease among the people"* (KJV). While this particular passage sets the stage for healing as an important part of Christ's ministry, other passages stress the importance of faith as the basis of such healing.

In Christ's healing of the woman with a blood problem (Mark 5:34; Luke 8:48), it is clearly stated that it was her faith that healed her. In like manner, it was the faith of the individual (or those assisting him) that served as a basis for Christ's restoring of

Bartimaeus' sight (Mark 10:52), the healing of the leper (Luke 17:19), and the healing of the paralytic (Mark 2:5; Luke 5:20). It is of interest to note that, in the case of the woman with the blood problem, she had been under the care of many doctors and had gotten worse, not better prior to seeking out Christ (Mark 5:26). This care may, very well, have included the use of herbal drugs available in Bible times.

Are we to interpret this as a ringing endorsement of faith healing and a condemnation of medical treatment? I don't believe so. Rather, it appears to be a statement of Christ's power over all things, including those that cannot always be cured by medicine. I do not believe that any thinking Christian would deny that Christ had and still has more power than all the resources of man. After all, we are told that by Him (Christ) all things are held together (Col. 1:17) and are sustained (Heb. 1:3).

It is quite clear from Scripture (particularly the book of Acts) that the gift of healing was passed on to the apostles. The first example of an apostolic miracle was the healing of the lame man by Peter (Acts 3:6-8). While there is no specific mention of the lame man's faith, his reaction to being healed (leaping and praising God) might suggest that his heart had been prepared for such an occasion and that he had faith.

Numerous additional accounts of healing by Peter and Paul are given in the book of Acts, but most of them do not indicate whether the healing was in response to the faith of the recipient or merely a demonstration of apostolic power in proclaiming the name of Christ. However, we are told in one case that Paul healed a crippled man because of his faith (Acts 14:9-10). How typical this case is, we are not told.

As pointed out by Unger,[3] the classic passage of Scripture on healing through prayer and faith is James 5:14-16. This passage challenges the elders of the church to pray for the sick among them and to anoint them with oil in the name of the Lord. We are told: *"And the prayer offered in faith will make the sick person well; the Lord will raise him up. If he has sinned, he will be forgiven"*

(James 5:15, NIV). Since this passage is addressed to believers, we can assume that faith and prayer are practiced on the part of the recipient of healing as well as by the elders.

One final point about biblical faith healing. We know that both faith and healing are gifts of the Holy Spirit (I Cor. 12:9). The question is, "Are such gifts confined to Bible times or are they meant to continue into the current age?" While some gifts of the Holy Spirit were confined to Bible times, no such declaration is made concerning healing gifts.[4] This being the case, there would appear to be a clear biblical basis for faith healing in the present Church age. However, the degree to which such current practices reflect Scriptural truths is a different issue.

Faith Healing in Contemporary Society

The faith healing movement of recent times is part of the broader and more comprehensive prosperity gospel.[5] In short, such a gospel states that prosperity and divine healing are the **rights** of every Christian who will appropriate enough faith to receive them. The key to prosperity and faith healing, then, becomes the ability to appropriate sufficient faith. How does one appropriate such faith? Apparently, this is done by making a "positive confession"—that is, to state in faith what you desire from God and believe that God will do it.[6] This, of course, includes healing of the physical body from all sorts of infirmities.

Conversely, one might assume that the Christian who is not healed is unable to exercise proper faith or may even be out of God's will. Carried to the extreme, this view concludes that sickness is caused by unbelief and sin.[7]

The father of the contemporary faith healing movement is widely acknowledged to be Kenneth Hagin.[8] While his views on faith healing were influenced by several evangelical and Pentecostal predecessors, he, more than anyone else, epitomizes the movement. Hagin was born in 1917 with a serious birth defect and, as a youngster, struggled through one debilitating circumstance after another. As a teenager, he was bedridden and physically paralyzed, often unable to maintain consciousness. However, as a result of praying and studying the Bible, he experienced a miraculous recovery. This recovery launched his ministry and belief in divine healing. His views on "positive confession"—our faith determines what we get from God—have been the mainstay of his ministry.

For one thing, the "positive confession" doctrine of healing is based upon a misunderstanding of Christ's atonement.[9] It assumes that the purpose of the atonement was to provide physical healing as well as forgiveness of sin. Yet, nowhere in Scripture do we find the promise of health or healing being given to the believer. In fact, the New Testament tells us that Paul and his associates experienced numerous illnesses. Are we to assume that **their** faith was too weak for God to heal them? No, I don't believe so.

Secondly, the "positive confession" doctrine of healing makes the sovereign God a human servant.[10] In this case, faith becomes a formula for success and God is obligated to deliver upon request. This view of God is heretical and certainly is not the God of the Bible. As one author puts it, God is reduced to a kind of "cosmic bellhop," attending to our needs.[11] This view leads to human pride and totally misinterprets the designed relationship established between God and the believer.

Finally, the "positive confession" doctrine tends to degrade those who are ill or poor by claiming that their condition is due to a lack of faith.[12] As if being ill weren't bad enough, these individuals are now burdened with guilt feelings about their lack of faith. Again, such a view is totally inconsistent with Scriptural teachings. Contrary to the assumptions of "positive confession," faith healing does not always take place.

What, then, can be concluded about the contemporary faith healing movement? On the positive side, we can thank the movement for helping the Church to reclaim its healing ministry.[13] For too long, the healing ministry has been ignored by traditions within the evangelical church and such practices have disappeared. Again, there is reason to believe that the "gift of healing" is alive and that God can, if He chooses, use such gifts to fulfill His will and purposes. On the more negative side, the contemporary faith healing movement has reinforced, even further, the Christian attitude mentioned earlier in the chapter. While most in the faith healing movement stop short of condemning medicine, they consider its use a sign of weak faith.[14] Medicine becomes a crutch to lean on until you get your "faith act" together.

The interesting thing about this view is that it is not just popular among those who actually practice faith healing, but that it has permeated the entire Christian community. Televangelism has brought the public demonstration of faith healing into our living rooms. While such marketing of faith healing frequently borders on charlatanry, the average Christian is still mesmerized by the prospect of God working in such dramatic ways. This, consciously or unconsciously, can increase their resistance to traditional medicine and cause them to examine their own faith. It is also the case that such resistance to traditional medicine has encouraged some Christians (particularly young Christians) to develop an interest in other forms of non-traditional treatments which border on the occult.[15]

The Medical Treatment Model

The medical treatment model is based upon the assumption that a specific illness exists and is best treated by some medically condoned remedy. In a typical application, the model makes the following assumptions:[16]

First, a patient appears with a **set of symptoms** and, on the basis of these symptoms, **a diagnosis is made.** In order for this diagnosis to be understood by and communicated to other medical professionals, it is identified as **a particular disease** from which the patient is suffering. Once the disease has been specified, **a cause can hopefully be determined** (so-called etiology). Typically, the cause is rooted in some well-defined **biological**

abnormality such as an infection or chemical imbalance. In instances where the abnormalities are not so well defined, the term "soft signs" may be used to cover a multitude of ambiguities. Finally, **a cure is recommended** to the patient based upon the real or assumed causes.

The medical treatment model is neatly packaged for the public's consumption and backed by the prestige of the medical professions. While there is widespread acceptance of this model by the general public, some Christians, as has been previously mentioned, find it difficult to accept unquestioningly such a natural, rather than supernatural, view of human behavior. After all, the medical treatment model is based exclusively on a physical view of life, whereas the Christian model is based upon a spiritual view of our relationship with God. Furthermore, to suggest that the two views really are not as different as they seem is no help at all. They are different—very different. However, it is important for us to recognize that God is equally interested in our physical and spiritual natures (1 Thess. 5:23).

While the primary purpose of Scripture is to address our spiritual needs, the Bible also has much to say about our bodies (see Chapter 4). Also, there is no indication in his writing that Luke the physician (Col. 4:14, KJV) experienced any spiritual conflict as a result of his medical training. Believe it or not, there are some physicians who are able to live a vital Christian life while addressing both the physical needs of their profession as well as the spiritual needs of their personal life. In fact, one of the most mature Christians I have ever met is a dear friend of many years who just happens to be a medical doctor.

It is time for Christians to recognize that God not only can use the lives of physicians as a testimony to His grace, but can also use the tools of their profession as a blessing to our lives. The medically supervised use of drugs is such a tool and can bring needed help or cure to the lives of Christians as well as non-Christians.

Having established the fact that the proper use of drugs is an integral part of the medical treatment model, how, then, are they used? It would appear that drugs are used for two specific purposes—to cure and to control symptoms. In some instances, the disease associated with a patient's illness is the result of a specific viral or bacterial infection of the body. The use of an appropriate drug leads to the killing of the virus or bacteria and rids the body of the disease. For example, the disease of syphilis, which is caused by the presence of spirochetes, can be cured with the use of an appropriate antibiotic. The important feature of such a curative role of drugs is that they not only treat the symptoms but correct the underlying problem as well. The cause of the disease is thus eliminated. The curative role of drugs best fits the assumptions of the medical treatment model by returning the patient to full health.

In other instances, the disease or disorder associated with a person's illness may be the result of complex or even unspecified causes. While we may know something about thc underlying problem, that may not be enough to eliminate (cure) the disease or disorder. Such is frequently the case with mental disorders like depression and schizophrenia. However, even in such cases, certain drugs can be effective in controlling symptoms of the disorder, if not in curing it. While the patient still has the disorder, the ability to control symptoms enables the patient to live a reasonably normal life. For example, treating schizophrenia with antipsychotic drugs enables the patient to live at home without actually eliminating the disorder. Furthermore, the fact that such drugs are effective in controlling the symptoms of a disorder gives scientists great hope that a more accurate cause of the disorder may some day be found, possibly leading to a cure.

The medical treatment model is not without its difficulties and problems, however. Some people criticize the indiscriminate practice by some physicians of prescribing drugs to patients without following their progress. This can be a very serious problem, particularly in those instances where the patient may be seeing more than one physician. The indiscriminate prescribing of drugs by any physician sets the stage for the potential abuse of prescription drugs and, in fact, puts the physician in the role of a "pusher." Fortunately, this practice is not widespread and most physicians monitor such activities carefully.

Others criticize the medical treatment model for its insensitivity to the importance of social and psychological factors in causing illness. In fact, some in the medical profession have been accused of "medicalizing" certain behavioral disorders that have no clear basis in biological conditions. For example, while the medical profession may treat a child's Attention Deficit Hyperactivity Disorder with drugs, some non-medical professionals believe that such a behavioral problem may have its roots in social-development problems, not in biology. If such is the case, drug treatment of the condition may be inappropriate as well as unnecessary.

In spite of such criticism, Christians should view the services rendered by the medical treatment model in a more positive light. The tools of the model (including the proper use of drugs) can be God's instrument of blessing in the lives of our children as is seen in the case of Carol.

Carol was a teenager who had been struggling with the debilitating disorder of cerebral palsy since birth. She was able to get around in a wheelchair and keep up with her class work at school. However, on occasions of stress (particularly exam time), she would experience a "seizure aura" or actually have a seizure. On one such occasion, she had a major seizure (convulsions with partial loss of consciousness) in the classroom and required assistance from the school nurse.

While Carol's parents were Christians, they accepted the fact that God had not chosen to heal Carol of her physical handicap and welcomed their doctor's recommendation that she take an anticonvulsant drug to control her seizures. The success of the medication in reducing the severity and frequency of Carol's seizures was accepted by her parents as God's provision and blessing in their lives.

Conclusion: A Balanced Perspective

It is important for Christians to realize that drugs are not intrinsically good or bad: it is their use that characterizes "good" or "bad." Abuse of drugs is "bad" in any form, whether it involves prescription drugs or those peddled on the street. By contrast, the proper medical use of drugs is "good" when it cures or alleviates debilitating symptoms. This point needs to be emphasized repeatedly when discussing drugs with young people.

Part of the problem some Christians have with the medical treatment model is due to the fact that they fail to make such a distinction. Because of the widespread focus on problems of drug abuse, we tend to miss or ignore the fact that an equal number of drugs are used to benefit society. We tend to see drugs, in general, as the encapsulation of the devil, himself, rather than realizing that it is **the improper use** of the drug that constitutes the potential "evil". In such cases, drugs get a bad rap.

When Christians, then, are confronted with the use of drugs in the medical treatment model, they have difficulty shedding the "negative baggage" associated with over-exposure to problems of drug abuse. This, coupled with the fact that many Christians see the acceptance of any medical treatment as a confirmation of their weak faith, causes them to shy away from the medical use of drugs. Hopefully, this chapter will help Christians (young and old) to re-examine their "negative baggage" associated with drugs and encourage them to develop a more balanced perspective on the "good" and "bad" uses of drugs.

A final word about faith and drugs as instruments of healing would also seem to be in order. As Christians, we have a rich and biblically-based heritage of faith healing. In spite of some contemporary abuses of this heritage, let's not, as the proverbial saying goes, "Throw the baby out with the bathwater." There is much of this heritage that should be salvaged, while recognizing the need to clean up our act. We need to get back to the biblical principles which serve as a foundation for such gifts of the Spirit and take it out of the realm of entertainment. As pointed out by Unger,[17] such gifts are more appropriately practiced in the privacy and fellowship of a local church.

By the same token, it is hoped that the Christian's acceptance of faith healing would not close his mind to the reality of and need for medically-supervised drug treatment. The two approaches do not need to be seen as contradictory or in competition. Rather, they supplement each other in God's plan for our lives. He can and frequently does use both as a means of blessing. Let's pass this message on to our young people and pray that they, too, might develop a balanced perspective on drugs.

Key questions answered by this chapter include:

1. Why do Christians resist natural means of healing?
2. Does faith healing have a sound biblical basis?
3. How is faith healing characterized in contemporary society?
4. What is the doctrine of "positive confession"?
5. Should Christians accept the medical use of drugs?
6. What beneficial purposes are served by the medical use of drugs?
7. Do the medical benefits of drugs require a denial of faith healing?

Notes

Chapter Seven

Drugs and the Law

Although Tammy was raised in a Christian home, she had been rebellious and difficult to discipline since her adoption at age two. When starting high school, she got in with the wrong crowd and started using drugs. One evening during summer vacation, she attended a party at a friend's house and participated in an all night PCP marathon. While still under the influence of the drug, she proceeded to steal a friend's car and drive irrationally through the busy streets of her neighborhood.

Fortunately, she did not have an accident or injure anyone in the process. However, she was soon arrested for stealing the car and driving under the influence of an illegal substance and was taken to the local police station. When arriving at the police station, she physically assaulted several policemen and, after a major struggle, was restrained and put into a "holding tank" at the station. When her mother arrived at the station she accompanied Tammy and two policemen to the local hospital where a drug test was administered.

Tammy tested positive for PCP and was returned to the police station until someone from the County Youth Authority arrived and transported her to the local Youth Detention Center. She remained in the Center over the weekend and was ordered to appear (with her parents) before a judge in juvenile court on Monday morning. While in court, Tammy continued to show disdain and disrespect for all authority and informed the judge that she would be out of the Detention Center before midnight of that day. The judge informed her that she was mistaken and sentenced her to 30 days of detention under tight security. Obviously, she did not leave that night or any other night during the 30-day period.

Such defiance of all authority (parents, police, judge) and disrespect for the law are typical of teenagers who abuse drugs. Drug laws are designed to protect young people and, when they ignore them, disaster strikes them and those with whom they associate. By contrast, respect for drug laws goes a long way in discouraging drug abuse.

The purpose of the present chapter is two-fold:

- to examine biblical teachings regarding the responsibility Christians have toward authority and the law; and

- to encourage Christians to obey and support the drug laws of our country.

Are Christians more likely to obey the law than non-Christians? Before you respond in the affirmative, let me phrase the question in more personal terms. Do you ever park illegally in a clearly marked handicap space in order to save a few steps at the supermarket or your favorite restaurant? Do you routinely and deliberately exceed the speed limit to and from your place of employment or even while running errands? Do you ever cut corners on your federal income tax return in order to save a little bit on the dreaded tax burden we all share? These questions are very poignant and have a clear bearing on the manner in which we live out our Christian testimony on a day-to-day basis.

Before my wife and I were married, she was involved in a children's home mission program in one of the Southern states. A colleague of hers named Tom, well known for his dedication to the mission program, was also notorious for his propensity to exceed the speed limit and, upon occasion, even to drive dangerously. Of course, he claimed that all of this was done in the name of expediting his duties in the cause of Christ. As is true with many Christians, he also thought that the "Jesus Saves" bumper sticker displayed on his car might be an effective way of giving testimony to his faith and ministering to those with whom he was unlikely to have any direct contact.

On one of his many driving escapades, he exercised the rare act of coming to a full stop at a traffic light. According to the story told to my wife, a total stranger pulled alongside of his car, rolled down his window and bellowed out in an unflattering tone, "You may be a Jesus man, but you drive like the devil." Instead of such comments piercing Tom's conscience, he laughed off the encounter and proceeded to drive in his usual manner. Furthermore, his solution to the problem and his strategy for avoiding such encounters in the future were most unusual. Upon returning to the mission headquarters, he removed his "Jesus Saves" bumper sticker from his car rather than considering the manner in which he drove to be the problem.

"What a strange response," you say. Perhaps, but how many of us also fail to see the relationship between our general respect for the law and our Christian testimony. If we fail to see the relationship, how can we expect our children to do so?

Biblical Teachings on Respect for the Law

The Bible is very clear in what it says about the Christian's responsibility to respect civil authority and to obey the laws established by such authority (Mark 12:17; Rom. 13:1-7; I Peter 2:13-17). A more detailed examination of biblical passages indicates both the nature and purpose of such authority over Christians as well as the consequences of disobedience to such authority.

- First of all, we are told to submit ourselves to authority because all authority is established by God and is the servant of God (Rom. 13:1,4). This includes authority at all levels of government—local as well as national (I Peter 2:13-14).

While we may have our doubts that certain persons in positions of authority over us have God's blessing, the general principle still holds. All authority (regardless of its moral fiber or political affiliation) is ordained by God as a form of established human order. Furthermore, as the servant of God, established authority serves as His instrument of reward and punishment to those under its jurisdiction (Rom. 13:3-4; I Peter 2:14). This is also the context in which specific community services such as the fire and police departments operate under the full authority of biblical guidelines. Again, the issue is not the degree to which persons in positions of authority fulfill their obligations in a responsible and equitable manner, but one of principle. Corruption in the local police department does not change God's ordained method of restraining corrupt or illegal behavior in human society.

- Secondly, we are told that to rebel against authority is to rebel against God Himself and will bring judgment upon the offender (Rom. 13:2).

As Christians, we want to be particularly careful that our displeasure and criticism of authority does not turn into rebellion. If it does, we are guilty of sinning against God, not simply our neighbor. While the context of this statement would also seem to imply that it is referring mainly to judgment by human authority, it is reasonable to assume that it is referring to the judgment of God as well. Such a conclusion is based upon the strong personal identification God makes with His instrument of human authority. Unfortunately, the threat of judgment and punishment (either now or later) is not a particularly strong motivator to the non-believer. However, it is hoped that believers (young and old) will see their submission to human authority as an act of worship and expression of love for God.

- Thirdly, we are told that we should submit to authority as a matter of conscience, not merely because of the threat of punishment (Rom. 13:5).

Submitting to human authority because of the threat of being punished if you break the law is not wrong in itself. Indeed, most non-believers and possibly many believers as well, operate at this level of conformity. However, it is hoped that the Christian submits to human authority for a more noble reason—that of conscience. We should submit to authority because we recognize that it is the right thing to do and our love for God compels us to seek His will and obey His statutes.

An example of the Christian's basis for submission is illustrated in Kohlberg's "stages of moral development".[1] In the early years of development, children respond mainly to reward and punishment and operate at what Kohlberg calls the "pre-conventional level" of morality. As individuals mature and become adolescents and adults, they tend to respond in ways that are expected by the general society and to develop values that are consistent with such societal standards. This is what Kohlberg refers to as the "conventional level" of morality. However, there are those adult individuals who operate at the level of what Kohlberg calls the "post-conventional" level of morality. These are individuals whose behavior and value system are guided by principles (matters of conscience), not merely by threat or the need to conform. Hopefully, the Christian's submission to human authority is based upon principles related to spiritual truths. While Kohlberg's theory of morality is based more on principles of justice (equality, fairness, etc.) than on Christian ethics, it still provides a clear example for Christians to emulate.[2]

- Finally, it is of interest to note that Christ, in spite of the oppressive nature of the Roman Empire and its rulers, demonstrated His submission to human authority and legitimized the subsidizing of such authority by taxation (Mark 12:17).

It is also important to note that Paul and other Christians of the first century did not revolt against the Roman government, no matter how hostile it became. Particularly during the time of Nero, many Christians were tortured and murdered, possibly including Paul himself.[3] Unfortunately, such examples of biblical submission to authority have been lost or repressed in today's social debates. Civil disobedience by Christians of all ages, particularly in those extreme cases where an individual destroys property or takes a life, only hurts the cause of Christ and His Kingdom.[4] The Scriptural command to submit to human authority **requires** that Christians work "within the system" to bring about social change.

Our young people, in particular, need to heed this admonition. These teachings have a direct bearing on the Christian's response to such policies.

Current Drug Laws

The Food and Drug Administration (FDA) oversees the manufacturing and distribution of drugs prior to their availability to the public.[5] The purpose of this oversight is to ensure the safety and effectiveness of the drug. The entire process is quite involved and, even if things go smoothly, may take years to achieve.

Once a drug has been made available for general use, it comes under the jurisdiction of the Controlled Substance Act of 1970 (see Appendix B for more detail on this Act). Drug use and abuse laws that are presently in effect are established and implemented by this Act.[6] This Act further provides for the levying of penalties for abuse based upon the particular schedule to which the drug has been assigned and the frequency of the violation. The principal federal agency responsible for enforcing these regulations is the Drug Enforcement Administration (DEA).[7] While the DEA is concerned mainly with the domestic enforcement of drug laws, it has, on occasion, also cooperated with the law enforcement agencies of other countries in the interdiction (cutting off or destroying) of drug sources.

The relevancy of Scriptural teachings regarding the Christian's submission to authority becomes immediately obvious when considering the nature of drug laws and their enforcement. For the Christian, drug laws should be seen as an instrument of God's servant—federal **authority.** Again, acceptance of such a view has absolutely nothing to do with our approval of how the federal government is being run or with the moral character of those in power. In spite of these factors, such drug laws are designed for our protection and the welfare of our children. If we abide by such laws, they become the instruments of reinforcement as well as God's blessing by the positive effect they have on our lives. However, if we violate such laws, they quickly become the instrument of punishment. Open rebellion against such drug laws must be viewed by the Christian as rebellion against God Himself and will certainly bring judgment in one form or another.

It is also obvious that, as Christians, we should obey drug laws for reason of **conscience,** not simply because we are threatened with fines or imprisonment if we violate them. Viewing drug laws in the light of Scriptural teachings regarding the Christian's submission to authority should give us a new respect and appreciation for the role they play in our everyday lives. Without such laws, our lives would be constantly threatened by the potential harm and destruction brought about by free access to such substances. As Christian adults, we should be strong supporters of all efforts (local and national) to enforce drug laws and should resist social pressure to change such laws simply because they appear not to work. Furthermore, we should pass these values on to our children in order that they, too, might develop a proper respect for drug laws.

While drug laws might be viewed as an instrument of God's ordained authority, they are, nevertheless, influenced by a number of practical issues related to drug abuse. These issues might be summarized in the following questions:[8]

- Should a person abusing a drug be treated as a criminal or as a sick person having a disease?

- How should the user (usually the victim) be distinguished from the pusher (supposedly the real criminal)? Who should be more harshly punished?

- Are the drug laws and their accompanying penalties effective deterrents against the illegal use or abuse of drugs?

In regard to the first issue, there is a sense in which drug abuse might legitimately be considered both a crime and an illness. Whenever a law makes the abuse of a drug illegal, a crime is committed when this law is broken. In this sense, all violations of drug laws (regardless of the reason) constitute **criminal acts** by the abuser. However, the primary characteristic of a criminal act of drug abuse in a conventional sense is the intent of the abuser. Such acts are deliberate, purposive, and show little regard for the welfare of others. It is in this sense that considering drug abuse a crime requires that the abuser be held to a high level of accountability.

In contrast to looking at drug abuse simply as a crime, there is some evidence (particularly in the case of alcoholism and possibly other drugs) that some individuals are genetically predisposed to drug abuse.[9] In this case, drug abuse takes on the characteristic of a disease, not a choice. Some individuals would go so far as to say that such a genetic predisposition provides an excuse for the drug abuse and that such individuals should not, therefore, be held responsible for their actions. However, at some point, the element of choice still enters the picture and it is doubtful that such individuals should be held to a lower level of accountability than the criminal abuser. From a Scriptural viewpoint, it is also possible that viewing drug abuse as a sickness (rather than a criminal act) simply provides excuses for ungodly behavior (Rom. 2:15). If our desire is to see that drug laws are implemented fairly and equitably, we want to be sure that we do not succumb to arguments that might deter us from such objectives.

In regard to the second issue, it is reasonably safe to say that drug laws have always been more lenient on the user than on the pusher of an abused drug. Since many drug abusers indulge in both activities, it may, in some instances, be hard to separate user from pusher. However, because of the high profits involved in drug trafficking and the need to keep a clear head, many pushers do not use the drugs they peddle. The law tries to focus on these individuals and holds them to a higher level of accountability than they do the user. The basic intent of such a focus is to get at the source of the drug supply. Unfortunately, the pervasive nature of organized crime operating behind the scenes makes it extremely difficult to penetrate the source of the drug beyond the level of the pusher.

It is also of interest to note that Scripture appears to hold the pusher to a higher level of accountability. In Luke 17:1, we are told, *"Things that cause people to sin are bound to come, but woe to that person through whom they come"* (NIV). It would appear that such a warning aptly describes the relationship of the drug pusher to the drug abuser.

In regard to the third and final issue, it would appear that federal drug laws have had only limited success in deterring the problem of drug abuse in our society. As to why this is the case, there may be numerous factors affecting the success of such laws, the most notable one of these being the general problem of supply and demand. As long as there is a public demand for drugs, there is going to be someone who is willing and able to supply such drugs. Attempts to interdict illegal drug supplies from other countries have been extremely costly and relatively ineffective.[10] Furthermore, when the source of drugs from one country is reduced, another source is waiting in the wings to fill the gap.

There is equally discouraging news in terms of attempts to curtail the demand side of the equation. It is the general failure of the federal drug laws to solve the problem of supply and demand that has led some individuals to call for a repeal of our present drug laws and a legalizing of controlled substances. However, such compromising of the lives of our children and young people would seem to be totally inconsistent with biblical principles. Rather, we need to strengthen current drug laws while, at the same time, recognizing the critical need for accompanying treatment programs.

We must also recognize that any attempt to legislate the behavior of the drug abuser is only going to be partially successful because of man's basic nature (Jer. 17:9; Mark 7:21-22; Rom. 3:23). Only a change in one's heart brought about by the power of God will, in the long run, change such behavior.

The Special Case of Marijuana

While the legal status of most drugs regulated by the Controlled Substance Act is clear, the legal status of marijuana may appear to be less so from the public's perspective. For one thing, the Act originally classified marijuana as a "Schedule 1" drug, which clearly implies that it has no recognizable medical use and has an extremely high potential for abuse. While the drug's abuse potential is dealt with elsewhere (Chapter 12), it has become increasingly clear that the drug has several beneficial medical uses.[11] These include the treatment of the side effects produced by chemotherapy in cancer patients and the reduction of fluid pressure in the eyes of glaucoma patients. However, attempts to get the DEA to re-schedule the drug, thus making it more readily available for medical use, have failed.

At the other end of the spectrum are those individuals who violate the laws regulating marijuana use and treat them as nothing more than a common nuisance. In addition, many young people are convinced that the government has been lying to them about the drug and its potentially deleterious effects. As a result of such developments, both liberals and conservatives have provided some support for the idea of not declaring marijuana legal, but making its possession a civil offense, punishable only by a fine. In the 1970's, several states actually decriminalized the use of marijuana, substituting civil fines of up to $100 in place of criminal penalties.[12] However, the 1980's saw the introduction of the "get tough" policies of the Reagan administration, and these policies killed any hope of the federal government decriminalizing the use of marijuana.[13] As a result, the pendulum has definitely swung back to a tougher stance on the possession and use of all illegal drugs, marijuana being no exception.

In spite of its potential medical use and attempts to decriminalize its use, the actual legal status of marijuana has not changed at all. It was and still is a "Schedule 1" drug with all of the legal ramifications associated with such a classification. Attitudes regarding the use of marijuana have changed over the years, and such changes may, in the long run, result in modifications in the legal status of the drug. However, we must deal with the law as it presently stands.[14] Thus, it would be inappropriate to encourage Christians to treat marijuana laws any differently than they would the laws regulating other illegal drugs. Respect and submission to marijuana laws are no less appropriate than is the case with laws regulating other drugs. We need to stress this fact with our young people.

Conclusion

The ungodly humanistic society in which we live tends to view drug laws in an entirely different manner than that which should characterize the Christian's view. Our secular society lacks a solid moral basis for making decisions and exercising personal discipline. Thus, when it comes to drug laws, many members of our society (particularly young people) are likely to see them as a hindrance to the fulfillment of personal desires and pleasures. Such individuals are also the primary force behind numerous social pressures to liberalize, and even eliminate, drug laws. At best, some of these individuals may tolerate drug laws for practical reasons or out of expediency, certainly not on the basis of principle. Evidence of such influences operating in our society is clearly seen in the open abuse of illegal drugs on our streets, the lack of social pressure to curb such activity, and the constant legal pressures to "lighten up" on the prosecution of drug offenders.

In contrast, the Christian has a solid moral basis for making decisions and exercising personal discipline—the Word of God. Since the Bible teaches Christians to respect authority, we see drug laws as an extension and instrument of God's appointed human authority and not something to rebel against. The fulfillment of selfish personal desires and pleasures takes a back seat to our desire to obey the statutes of God and to fulfill His purpose in our lives. Such a view based upon Scriptural principles should motivate the Christian to be in the vanguard of support for drug laws.

Even if Christians fail to see the importance of supporting drug laws for their own sake, hopefully they will, at least, see the importance of such support for the sake of their children. We most certainly cannot expect our children to demonstrate a respect for drug laws if we are unwilling to practice such respect in our own lives. Christians should also be thankful that there is still enough godly influence in high places of government to presently sustain such laws. How long this will continue to be the case is unclear.

In addition to the previous emphasis on the deleterious effects of drugs on the Christian's body and mind, the Christian's responsibility to abide by drug laws (based upon biblical teachings) is another valid reason for avoiding the abuse of drugs. Indeed, such a reason would stand on its own merit, quite apart from any other arguments. Hopefully, our young people will also see this as a valid reason for avoiding the abuse of drugs.

Key questions answered by this chapter include:

1. Should a Christian's testimony reflect respect for the law?
2. What does the Bible teach about responsibility toward authority?
3. How should Christians view current drug laws in our society?
4. What are some practical issues raised by current drug laws?
5. Are drug laws effective deterrents against drug abuse?
6. Have drug laws related to marijuana changed?
7. Do Christians have a moral basis for upholding drug laws?

Notes

Chapter Eight

Drugs and the Christian Home

While having no specific evidence that Bob was, in fact, experimenting with drugs, his parents thought it best to tackle the matter without delay. As is true with so many Christian parents, they approached the situation with the best of intentions and sincerely desired to warn Bob about the dangers of using drugs. However, rather than discussing such matters with him in an open and honest atmosphere, their warning about the use of drugs usually turned out to be a dogmatic and unsympathetic monologue on the consequences of such practices. Little sensitivity was expressed for the struggles and temptations young people face in today's society. Usually the monologue went something like this, "Drugs will drive you crazy" or, "Stay away from drugs, they'll kill you."

Without intending to do so, his parents cut off all opportunity for listening to Bob's concerns and learning about the specific nature of his personal struggle with drug issues. After listening to several such lectures by his parents, Bob realized that they knew little or nothing about drugs or the struggle young people face, and that his friends were a much better source of information than they were. Unfortunately, in Bob's case, it was too late for his parents to have any impact and the door had been closed to the possibility of a constructive discussion about drugs with him.

Fortunately, however, two of Bob's close friends at school were also Christians and, with their support and encouragement, he was able to resolve drug issues on his own. While he did experiment with marijuana on two occasions while visiting the home of a non-Christian friend, in the final analysis, he decided that drugs were not going to get a hold on him.

Messages designed to frighten young people or which exaggerate the physical and psychological dangers of drugs usually don't work and frequently backfire on parents. In general, teenagers know more about drugs than do their parents and frequently base their decisions on such knowledge. The role of parents is to listen to, encourage, and support young people in their struggle against drugs, not dictate policy to them. In order to do this effectively, parents need to be informed about the effects and dangers of different drugs and speak openly and honestly about such issues. Bob's parents are an example of what not to do and of the failure of the Christian family to properly address the drug problem; however, they surely are not the exception.

The family is a microcosm of society and a good barometer of how well society functions. If the family is strong and functions well, society tends to reflect such stability in terms of its social and moral fiber. If, however, the family is redefined in non-traditional terms (e.g., single-parent household or same-sex parents) or is characterized by strife (dysfunctional qualities), these factors cannot help but have an impact on our society. All we have to do is look at the disintegration of the traditional family in our current society and see the impact it is having on the social and moral fiber of our communities. Even non-Christians recognize the critical relationship between the traditional family and society and are calling for a re-focusing on the importance of the family unit.

As Christians, we of all people should not be surprised by the critical role the family plays in society. After all, the family is God's ordained vehicle for teaching and passing on values to our children, with such values being the very substance that gives society its cohesiveness. The family is also the vehicle through which individual problems (including drug abuse) are best addressed and resolved. While various government agencies may fund all kinds of drug-abuse prevention and treatment programs, these programs are not the real solution to the problem. Rather, the solution lies in the character of the family and the degree to which it reflects God's rules of operation.

The present chapter has several objectives:

- to review biblical admonitions to the Christian family;
- to discuss characteristics of the drug-abuse family;
- to present some signs of teenage drug abuse that Christian workers and parents need to look for; and finally,
- to recommend a general game plan to help in dealing with drug abuse.

This chapter is not designed to make Christian parenting any easier; however, it is hoped that it will make Christian workers and parents more sensitive and responsive to problems of drug abuse in the family.

Biblical Admonitions to the Christian Home

If someone totally unfamiliar with our culture and society were to judge family structure and values by what they see on our prime-time television programs, they would be easily confused or mislead as to the meaning of family. The most common portrayal of family life is the struggling single parent balancing a full-time job with the raising of children or a multiple-adult household dividing up the responsibilities that would normally be assumed by the father and mother. One might ask, "What ever happened to family images captured in such television programs as 'Father Knows Best' or 'Ozzie and Harriet'?" Well, it is quite obvious that such wholesome images simply don't cut it in our society and are stereotypes of the past. However, God's plan for the family is clearly outlined in His Word, with each member's role and responsibility spelled out in detail. The nuclear family has three subsystems—parents, spouses and children—and admonitions are addressed to each.[1]

To parents, the Bible says that they are to teach godly principles to their children (Deut. 6:6-7) and to train them in the way they should go and when they are old, they will not depart from it (Prov. 22:6). Unfortunately, some parents treat the latter admonition as an invariant rule rather than a general principle. While early spiritual training is clearly important in forming a child's character, you may find an individual child who chooses to reject such training.[2] However, this does not negate the importance of the general principle of spiritual training by parents or excuse them for failing to implement such training.

It is also of interest to note that admonitions to the father are particularly strong. To him, the Bible says, *"Do not exasperate your children; instead, bring them up in the training and instruction of the Lord"* (Eph. 6:4, NIV). The fact that this admonition is addressed to the father rather than the mother or both parents is probably indicative of the difference in the temperament of men as well as reflective of the role of leadership and responsibility the father is to assume in the family. The latter view would seem to find support in the Bible's strong condemnation of the man who fails to provide or care for his immediate family (I Tim. 5:8).

The biblical admonitions to spouses are particularly critical since the relationship of husband and wife is the very backbone of the family. Wives are instructed to *"... submit to your husbands as to the Lord. For the husband is the head of the wife as Christ is the head of the church..."* (Eph. 5:22-23, NIV). This passage is not a license for husbands to treat their wives as inferior or as servants of their every passion but, rather, is designed to establish priorities in the family. The husband is likened to Christ as the head of the church and the wife has the obligation of acknowledging the husband's leadership role in the family. This role of leadership by the husband is a profound one and is accompanied by awesome responsibility. Husbands are told to *"... love your wives, just as Christ loved the church and gave himself up for her to make her holy..."* (Eph. 5:25-26, NIV). A simple reflection on such love should be enough to transform the husband's love and concern for his wife. Indeed, if the spouses recognize their true relationship to each other, there will be **a mutual submission** based upon their mutual reverence for Christ (Eph. 5:21).

To children, the biblical admonition is equally clear. They are instructed to *"... obey your parents in the Lord, for this is right..."* (Eph. 6:1, NIV). This admonition does not say that children are to obey their parents when they feel like it, nor does it provide any guarantee that parents are always right in their judgment. However, it does establish the line of authority within the family and make the children subordinate to the parents in all matters of importance. Such a position of subordination does, however, have its benefits in that children can expect to be protected and cared for by their parents as well as having some hope for the future (Eph. 6:3).

The family defined in biblical terms is a dynamic entity and a powerful force in establishing values (spiritual as well as general values) in children. Indeed it is the only entity that has the time and resources for doing so. Leaving the teaching of such values to other institutions in our society simply will not work. These other institutions do not have the children for a sufficient amount of time to do the job and, even if they did, parents would have no assurance their children were learning values consistent with biblical principles.

In the Christian home, it is important for parents to recognize that values are taught by their actions as well as by their words. In the present context, this refers to spiritual truths that are relevant to the problems of drug abuse. Parents need to **verbally** communicate to their children what the Bible teaches about the Christian's body and mind and how drug abuse can spoil God's plan for their young lives. Children also need to be reminded of what the Bible says about respect for the law and how breaking drug laws can lead not only to possible punishment but also can affect their access to future educational and business opportunities. Such verbal instructions should not be characterized by a single occasion of talking to the child but, rather, be a part of the extended interaction of the parents with their children (Deut. 6:7).

Christian parents cannot stop here but must also "practice what they preach" in a consistent manner. To say one thing (no matter how profound) and live by different rules presents conflicting messages to children and simply won't cut it. Children get enough conflicting messages outside of the family and look to the family for stability and consistency. Parents must **live by the values they teach** to their children. If there is a house rule against the use of drugs in any form (including alcohol or cigarettes), then parents must respect the rule for it to be effective. This is not the occasion for parents to exercise their freedom in Christ but, rather, to recognize the impact their behavior has on their children (1 Cor. 8:9-13). Parents simply have to recognize their children as the highest priority and be willing to make sacrifices for the sake of consistency. Nothing short of such a strategy will suffice.

Regarding the enforcement of drug rules in the home, it is important for parents to be both **consistent and reasonable** in such practices. Consistency requires that parents not only set rules but be willing to follow through with punishment if the rules are violated. The punishment should be commensurate with the violation and, above all else, parents should avoid unrealistic threats. To tell the children that you are going to "beat them half to death" serves no constructive purpose and the first time you fail to implement such an unrealistic threat, you have lost your disciplinary edge. The realistic punishment of social isolation or sacrifice is likely to be much more effective in the long run and allows the parents to exercise reasonable control over the situation.

Surprisingly, children may also respond to **reason**, and a brief explanation of the purpose for drug rules may go a long way in smoothing over the entire process of managing the situation.

The biblical picture of a Christian family provides all of us with a model to emulate. For those Christian families that are still intact (regardless of their present level of functioning), the biblical picture of a Christian family is a call to renewal and recommitment to godly principles. Only by responding to such a call will Christian parents be prepared to cope effectively with problems of drug abuse by their children.

However, the biblical picture of a Christian family also provides a clear diagnosis for the present spiritual illness of the family and its inability to deal with problems of drug abuse. The more a family deviates from the biblical model, the more difficult it becomes to implement the responsibilities and functions of the family subsystems. Such an assumption is not a condemnation of the single-parent family, but simply a recognition of the fact that one parent cannot serve both sex roles as effectively as can a husband and wife. When some single Christian parents do a good job of instilling spiritual values in their children, it is a testimony to God's grace and faithfulness in the face of adversity, not a negation of God's design for the family.

Characteristics of the Drug-abuse Family

The most prevalent characteristic of the drug-abuse family is the **pervasive nature** of the abuse problem. The family is a dynamic system and when something goes wrong in one part of the system it has a profound impact on all parts of the system.

This basic point was brought into focus for me many years ago when my wife and I were having problems with our adopted daughter. As a result of behavioral and emotional problems our daughter was seeing a psychologist, who just happened to be family-therapy oriented. While my wife was very accepting of her need to become part of the therapy process, I, on the other hand, was reluctant to do so. As I look back on this occasion, my reluctance was undoubtedly due to professional pride and my refusal to believe the problem was, in any manner, mine.

However, when I finally agreed to participate in the therapy process, I learned a profound lesson. I finally recognized the degree to which our daughter's problem had impacted both of us individually as well as how her problem had affected our marriage relationship.

So it is with a problem of drug abuse by a child in the family. What may start out to be a problem of drug abuse identified with a particular child rapidly becomes a problem for the whole family. Not only is each member of the family affected by the behavior of the abuser, but each member may also be required to make adjustments and undergo changes in seeking a solution to the problem. Indeed, things are never going to be quite the same and that is a result of the drug-abuse problem.

Another common characteristic of the drug-abuse family is the presence of **unfulfilled needs** on the part of the abuser.[3] The identification of such a characteristic may sound like a "cop-out" since everyone has needs that, from time to time, are not met. However, for the teenager, unmet needs are intensified and require special attention by parents.

Of all the needs experienced by teenagers, emotional needs are, undoubtedly, the most important.[4] While teenagers are sampling the adult world outside of the home, they need to be assured of their parents' love, support and acceptance. If these needs are not being adequately met, teenagers will seek satisfaction of their needs elsewhere—including experiencing drugs. Drug abuse is not only a powerful substitute for need satisfaction but also allows teenagers to temporarily escape the vacuum left by the parents' inattention to the problem.

The teenagers' experience of intimacy with the family is not only critical in satisfying their immediate needs, but also becomes the prototype of their potentially intimate relationship with God. As teenagers learn from their day-to-day relationship with parents that they are accepted and loved in spite of their actions, so they learn, too, that God loves and accepts them in spite of their disobedience. Of course, this lesson by analogy is effective only when the parents are, themselves, living close to God.

A third common characteristic of the drug-abuse family is that of **denial.**[5] Such a practice is common among drug abusers in that they simply do not want to face the music. After all, drug abuse can become a valuable crutch in the lives of teenagers and for them to recognize that they have a drug problem can be an extremely painful experience. Denial in this context can be clearly understood and is an effective defense mechanism for avoiding such a confrontation. However, the most interesting thing about denial in the family of a teenage drug abuser is that denial is not limited to the abuser. In fact, parents of a drug-abusing teenager also become experts at denial for many of the same reasons. To admit that their child has a problem with drug abuse clearly reflects on their parenting skills and creates feelings of inadequacy and shame. Denying that a drug problem exists allows them to avoid such self-debasing experiences.

In his book, Lutes relates one of the clearest examples of such denial by a father of a drug-abusing son.[6] Even after his son died from an overdose of cocaine and an autopsy proved the presence of the drug in the son's body, the father still refused to accept the fact that his son had died from drug abuse. Incredulous you say; well perhaps, but denial can be tremendously strong even when it is totally irrational. Breaking this cycle of denial within the drug-abuse family and recognizing that a problem exists must be the first step in seeking a solution to the problem.

A final common characteristic of the drug-abuse family is the **peripheral role played by the father.**[7] In some instances, the father is absent from the home as a result of divorce and sees the child only on limited and highly structured occasions. Such limited contact does not permit him to exercise his responsibility as a father. In other instances, the father may be present in the home but assumes a passive role and relegates the responsibility of child rearing to the wife. In either case, an important element of the family system is missing and the stability of the family unit is threatened.

While the absence of the father's influence may not directly **cause** problems of drug abuse, it can easily create a vacuum within which problems of discipline and control can develop. These problems can, in turn, result in teenagers within the family experimenting with drugs and eventually abusing them.

The general picture that emerges from the drug-abuse family is that of a serious misunderstanding of the **nature and extent** of the problem.[8] As a result, the reaction of parents to the problem tends to be inappropriate or insufficient. Christian parents have a real need to recognize the signs of drug abuse in their teenagers.

Signs of Teenage Drug Abuse

The major signs associated with drug abuse in teenagers can be conveniently grouped into four categories: behavioral changes, personality changes, physical changes, and changes in the choice of entertainment. Specific examples will be given for each of these categories which, hopefully, will serve as a kind of checklist for parents to apply to their individual situations.

Behavioral changes: Changes in behavior associated with drug abuse are likely to include a wide variety of deviations from the normal routine of teenagers.[9] While not all changes in friends are negative, a sudden and radical change in the circle of friends may be a danger sign. This may be especially true if the teenager spends his time with the new friends to the exclusion of other friends.

Another behavioral change associated with drug abuse may be a pattern of cutting classes and a significant deterioration in school performance. Since many things other than drug abuse may also affect the teenager's performance in school, Christian workers and parents need to be cautious about making an uninformed judgment on this matter.

Perhaps the most important behavioral change associated with teenage drug abuse is a deliberate attempt to avoid any serious contact or interaction with parents. Such avoidance of intimacy allows the teenager to minimize the possibility of giving off other "tell-tale" signs of drug abuse and should be a major red flag to parents.

Personality changes: Changes in personality associated with drug abuse are likely to be reflected in any drastic and sudden shift in the teenager's mood, attitudes, interests or values. If a teenager is depressed or vacillates significantly in his mood, such changes may be indicative of the "on and off" effects of drug abuse.[10] In a similar manner, if a normally cooperative teenager suddenly refuses to do things around the house to help parents, such an attitude shift may be a significant danger sign.

Such an attitude shift may also be expressed in a variety of changes in interests. The drug-abusing teenager is likely to show little interest in doing things as a family and is likely to seek interests outside of the home. Again Christian workers and parents need to be cautious about making a judgment on such changes without examining other potential influences in the lives of their teenagers.

A final personality change that Christian workers and parents should be very sensitive to is that associated with a basic shift in values. If, for example, a teenager suddenly loses all interest in spiritual matters or attending church, something other than superficial changes are taking place. Such basic changes in values often accompany drug abuse and require immediate attention.

Physical changes: Physical changes associated with drug abuse can take one of two forms—physical symptoms and physical appearance. Regarding the former, there are specific changes in the eyes such as pupillary dilation or constriction as well as general "blood-shot" features that are associated with drug abuse. Other physical symptoms associated with drug abuse may include changes in complexion color, problems of coordination and distorted perception, particularly depth perception.

Changes in physical appearance associated with drug abuse typically center around choice of clothing and attention to grooming. If teenagers dress as if they don't care how they look instead of merely trying to be faddish, such changes should not be ignored. If changes in dress are also accompanied by a decreased interest in general cleanliness and grooming, one needs to recognize the potential role of drug abuse in bringing about these changes. Since dress codes and grooming fashions are constantly changing with teenagers, Christian workers and parents need to be sensitive to such fads in order to assess the degree to which their teenager deviates from them.

Changes in choice of entertainment: One of the most frequent changes in choice of entertainment associated with drug abuse is that related to musical preference. In general, drug abusing teenagers are more likely to prefer hard rock, heavy metal or rap music over other types. Such music expresses the anger and frustration of a segment of our youth population and reinforces the "mindset" of the teenage drug abuser. Parents need to be aware of the entertainment choices of their teenagers and the degree to which such choices consume their recreational times.

Since heavy metal music, in particular, is often associated with the occult and satanism, Christian workers and parents also need to be sensitive to the role of symbolism in the life of the teenager. While a temporary interest in such matters may not be serious, strong attraction to satanic figures and symbols may accompany drug abuse.

While no one of the preceding categories of signs, by itself, is sufficient in identifying teenage drug abuse, collectively such signs can provide one more instrument in the family's battle against drug abuse.[11]

A Family Strategy and Concluding Comments

The Christian family is not immune to problems of drug abuse and needs a "game plan" for dealing with such problems. While details of the plan may differ with the specific circumstances surrounding the abuse, the following guidelines are offered as a general framework for such a plan:

Be realistic: Recognize the problem for what it is—a drug problem—no more or no less. While drug abuse is a serious problem, don't equate it with the end of the world or blow it out of proportion to its true seriousness. Chances are that you and your child will survive the ordeal and will be stronger as a result of the experience.

Be reasonable: Make the degree of response commensurate with the degree of the drug abuse problem. Above all else, don't overly theologize or spiritualize the problem of drug abuse.[12] Young people probably already feel badly enough about abusing drugs, without you accusing them of rejecting God and all that is holy by their actions.

Tackle the problem with love, support and forgiveness: Make a clear distinction between the problem of drug abuse and the child. The child **has** a problem but the child **is not** the problem. The Christian worker or parent who fails to make such a critical distinction is also likely to fail in the task of finding a solution to the problem. The children need to know that they are loved, cared for and accepted throughout the entire process.

Know when to seek professional help: Don't wait until the problem gets out of hand before you seek professional advice or help, preferably Christian. We will have more to say about available types of help and the importance of a Christian orientation in the next chapter.

A grandparent was once overheard to say, "If I had known grandparenting was so much fun, I would have by-passed parenting altogether." While we may laugh at such an impossible scenario for our lives, the statement does, indirectly, attest to the pain and frustration of parenting. Furthermore, the problem is only exacerbated by the presence of drug abuse in a teenage-family member.

In addition to all that has been said in this chapter, parents must also remember to **pray for their children** on a daily basis. It is not an easy life for teenagers and we need to bring our children and their problems before the Lord on a regular basis. The Lord is faithful and His promises are trustworthy (I Thess. 5:24; II Pet. 3:9); however, this does not mean that things will always work out the way we think they should.

Key questions answered by this chapter include:

1. In what way is the family a reflection of society?
2. What are the biblical admonitions to the Christian family?
3. How can biblical principles help the family deal with drug problems?
4. What are the characteristics of the drug-abuse family?
5. Why is the family problem of drug abuse so pervasive?
6. What are some specific signs of teenage drug abuse?
7. What signs of drug abuse are associated with satanic interests?
8. What guidelines provide a family strategy for drug problems?

Notes

Chapter Nine

Drug Treatment and Spiritual Healing

Peggy was a Psychologist who, in addition to her daytime position, worked two evenings a week in a church-sponsored counseling ministry. During this time, she had seen how tragedy strikes the lives of Christians in many of the same ways it does non-Christians. She recounted, in particular, the time she met with Joan in three different counseling sessions. Joan was a divorced mother with a small child to support and blamed God for her plight and economic devastation. Her ex-husband refused to send her child support on a regular basis and she had been unable to seek full-time work with the small child. Her part-time work (made possible by a friend helping out with the child) was barely enough to pay the rent on her small apartment and put food on the table.

While Joan was supposedly a Christian, she failed to see how calling upon the Lord in such a situation would change things. Despondence developed into depression over the situation and Joan would typically drink herself to sleep on cheap wine after putting the baby to bed in the evening. The stupor produced by the wine became Joan's temporary escape from the realities of her life and was the thing she most looked forward to at the end of the day. She finally realized she needed professional help and, recognizing that the counseling ministry might be more understanding of her financial situation, she ended up there.

In counseling and praying with Joan, Peggy was able to show her that Christian friends and God were very much a part of the solution to her problems. After three counseling sessions, a young married couple at the church took Joan under their wing and helped her get back on her feet spiritually and economically. It turned out that they were able to arrange free babysitting for Joan which enabled her to get a full-time job at a local store and turn her life around. Joan realized she did not need the booze anymore to escape reality or help her relax and sleep at night. Two months after the final counseling session, Joan informed Peggy that she was doing much better financially and had made some new friends at the church. Joan's final words to Peggy were, "I finally see how God was part of my recovery and I couldn't have done it without your help and that of Christian friends." Peggy's account of Joan's recovery is a clear example of how a solution to drug abuse (alcohol in this case) and spiritual healing go hand in hand.

If this chapter misses the mark, then all that has been said about biblical guidelines in the preceding six chapters becomes irrelevant. The mark is simply this: there must be a solution to the problem of drug abuse that integrates such information into a unique picture of treatment and healing—one that is biblical and distinctly Christian in nature. Although secular treatment models have served as a basis for Christian models, they are not enough. The Christian models must add the characteristics of human nature taught by Scripture and make them an integral part of both treatment and healing. Human nature being what it is, the only reasonable goal of drug treatment should be that of total abstinence.

While, to some secular theorists, the controlled use of drugs may appear to be an acceptable solution to the problem of drug abuse,[1] such a strategy is self-defeating and unacceptable to the Christian. The difference between "no use" and "some use" is monumental and as profound as the difference between day and night. However, the difference between "some use" and "abuse" is, at best, cloudy and, at worst, arbitrary, meaningless and indiscernible to the drug user.

With this perspective in mind, the purpose of the present chapter is:

- to discuss some general treatment models for chemical abuse,
- to demonstrate their Christian adaptations, and

- to emphasize the uniqueness of Christian treatment.

General Treatment Models

Probably the most widely recognized treatment program for chemical abuse in existence today is the 12-step program of Alcoholics Anonymous (AA). While the principles encompassed by this 12-step program are highly unique, the only basic requirement for its application is a sincere desire on the part of the individual to stop drinking. The uniqueness of this program is captured in several distinctive features.[2]

- First, it assumes that alcoholism is a disease.

However, the concept of "disease" is not used in a literal sense but, rather, in a metaphoric sense. That is to say, there is no insistence that alcoholism has its roots in physiology or genetic influences but only that the individual recognizes that they have no control over the problem and need help.

- Second, the AA program assumes that abstinence is required to deal with the disease.

The individual is encouraged to recognize the fact that once an alcoholic, always an alcoholic and to touch even one drink is flirting with disaster.

- Third, it is assumed that some higher power is an important part of the treatment/recovery process.

Such an assumption is clearly indicated by the fact that 7 of the 12 steps mention either God, prayer or spiritual awakening. It is, of course, recognized that the word "God" is couched in loose enough language to accommodate religious plurality. Accordingly, God is viewed as that person or power understood by the individual. It is of interest to note that, in spite of the flexible definition of God, many individuals still refuse to participate in AA because of its reference to God and a higher power.

As treatment programs go, AA has certainly had its fair share of success. While no one factor explains this success, several characteristics probably contribute to it.[3]

First of all, there is the characteristic of **mutual sharing** by the members of the AA group. Such sharing undoubtedly helps the individual recognize that he is not alone in his struggle and that his problem is not unique.

Second, there is the provision for **regular support** by the group as a whole and by an individual sponsor within the group. This is what is commonly known as the "buddy system". Furthermore, the sponsor provides a 24-hour-a-day crisis intervention link between the alcoholic and the AA group.

Third, AA meetings are scheduled **frequently and regularly** with the individual strongly encouraged to attend every meeting. Such availability and consistency of support is critical to the recovering alcoholic and helps to structure his life. In many instances, this may be the only structure in his life and, in turn, it may provide the basis for organizing other aspects of his life.

Finally, the fact that **no personal expenses** are involved in joining or attending AA makes the program a reasonable choice. Many individuals recovering from alcoholism probably do not have the money to pay for expensive treatment and find AA an attractive alternative for that reason.

A closer examination of the twelve steps of the AA program clearly indicates why it is so adaptable to Christian treatment programs, for prevalent themes running through the steps are loaded with spiritual meaning and implications. Such themes include: admission of being powerless, turning to God and humbly asking for His help, improving our consciousness of God through prayer, making amends, and carrying the message to others. We'll have more to say about these matters later in the chapter.

Other groups have also adapted the 12-step AA model for a variety of drug-related problems.[4] In some cases, this is to provide support for the families of recovering alcoholics. Such is the case with the group Al-Anon. As was indicated in the preceding chapter, drug abuse (including alcohol abuse) becomes a problem for the entire family and such a group recognizes the need to address this fact. Additional adaptations of the AA model include groups designed to treat heroin abuse (Narcotics Anonymous) and cocaine abuse (Cocaine Anonymous). It appears that the AA program is the cornerstone for a wide variety of treatment groups that are reaching an increasing number of people.

In contrast to the "self-help" nature of the AA treatment model is the more aggressive medical-intervention model. The medical approach to the treatment of drug abuse (alcohol as well as other drugs) involves two specific treatment phases—detoxification and aftercare.[5] Both of these phases will be briefly considered in order to demonstrate the difference in underlying philosophy of the medical approach.

Detoxification is a "first-line" intervention in drug abuse and describes the process by which the abused substance is cleared from the abuser's body. Withdrawal (either sudden or gradual) of the substance is required in this process and should, with few exceptions, be conducted under medical supervision. Since alcohol withdrawal can cause delirium tremors,[6] tranquilizers may be used to reduce the risk associated with such symptoms. However, with most substances, the painful process of withdrawal can be completed without the use of additional medication. Detoxification is a necessary preliminary step in most treatment programs (including AA), since recovery is defined in terms of "being off" and "staying off" the drug.

Once the individual has been "dried out," it becomes necessary to provide some long-term, follow-up treatment. In the medical model this is generally known as **aftercare.** A typical aftercare approach with alcoholics might include the use of the drug Antabuse. This drug blocks the enzyme that metabolizes alcohol and, as a result, causes the individual to become very sick. As long as the person stays on Antabuse, he is likely to avoid any use of alcohol. A similar aftercare approach with heroin abusers might include the use of drugs (e.g., Narcan or Trexan) that block the action of narcotics. These drugs will prevent relapse and, even if the individual did take heroin, it would have no effect. As is true with Antabuse, the success of opiate blockers depends upon the individual's faithfulness in taking them.

One interesting twist to the medical treatment model is the methadone treatment program.[7] In this case, the heroin abuser does not go through a detoxification phase at all. Rather, he is maintained on a substitute opiate drug called methadone. Such a maintenance program is medically supervised and, thus, avoids many of the peripheral activities (including crimes to acquire drugs) associated with drug abuse. However, the abuser never gets off the drug. Thus, the ultimate objective of this program is not abstinence as is the case with most aftercare treatment programs.

The AA and medical treatment models are not contradictory nor do they, necessarily, compete with each other. With one exception (methadone maintenance program), both models see abstinence as essential to the success of the program. Furthermore, neither AA nor medical aftercare can be implemented until the initial phase of detoxification has been completed. The twelve steps of the AA model is as much an aftercare program as is the second phase of the medical model and makes no sense unless the abuser is first of all "dried out". The one point at which they do differ is the underlying philosophy which motivates the success of the programs. AA is a "self-help" approach to treatment, whereas the medical model is an aggressive intervention program carried out by health professionals. As will become apparent in the next section, the flexible, loosely-structured nature of the AA model is more readily adapted to the treatment needs of the Christian community.

Christian Adaptation of the AA Model

The 12-step AA model has its roots in Christian tradition and the evangelical movement of the early 1900's.[8] Apparently, the twelve steps developed directly out of the evangelical practices of the Oxford group, a movement associated with the American Lutheran clergyman, Frank Buchman. This group stressed the importance of the conversion experience, as well as emphasizing prayer, mutual confession and making restitution.[9] It is no wonder, then, that prevalent themes running through the steps are loaded with spiritual meaning and implications. While much of the original spiritual emphasis may have been lost in today's pluralistic society, the 12-step AA program may still be the most important spiritual model for addressing abuse problems of contemporary Christians (both young and old).

Assuming this to be the case, two of the most influential adaptations of the 12-step AA approach to Christian treatment will be briefly considered. These include the *Roman Road to Recovery* of the Minirth-Meier group and the *Rapha's 12-step Program for Overcoming Chemical Dependency*. While both of these Christian treatment programs have a solid biblical basis, their use of Scripture differs in some significant ways.

The *Roman Road to Recovery* is a 12-step program of recovery from abuse that is based upon principles taken from the first fourteen chapters of the Book of Romans.[10] The essential features of this program are summarized in the following statements:

- We must recognize our helplessness, for we are all potential addicts (stages 1, 2, 3; Rom. 1: 16, 21, 24; Rom. 2: 16; Rom. 3: 20).

- We must recognize the power of faith, receive God's love, and relinquish self-ownership to God (stages 4, 5, 6; Rom. 4: 17; Rom. 5: 8, 9; Rom. 6: 13).

- We must reconstruct our pattern of living and take audit of ourselves (stages 7, 8; Rom. 7, 8, 9; Rom. 10: 9-11).

- We must restore broken relationships, replace our lifestyle, relieve others' burdens and reach out to others (stages 9, 10, 11, 12; Rom. 11: 22, 23; Rom. 12: 1, 2, 9; Rom. 13: 9, 10; Rom. 14: 15-17).

As is quite clear, many of the stages in this program parallel quite closely the twelve steps of the AA model. However, there is one important difference: the purpose of the present program is not only to deliver the abusers from their addiction but also to enable them to be used regularly by God as a vessel for communicating spiritual healing (as well as physical healing) to others.

As another Christian adaptation of the AA model, the *Rapha's 12-step Program for Overcoming Chemical Dependency* differs from the preceding one in two basic ways.[11]

First of all, there is a broader use of Scripture in support of the recovery process. This includes one reference to the Old Testament book of Lamentations as well as various references throughout the New Testament.

Secondly, while many of the same principles are incorporated into the recovery process, the steps are ordered in a slightly different manner. This will become apparent in the following summary of the essential features of the program:

- We admit to God, ourselves and others the nature of our wrongs and that our lives are powerless and unmanageable (steps 1,5;Rom.7:18,James 5:16).

- We turn our lives over to God seeking restoration, renewal of our minds, deliverance from sinful patterns of abuse, and the power to grow in our relationship with Jesus Christ (steps 2, 3, 6, 7, 11; Phil. 2: 13; Rom. 12: 1; James 4: 10; Rom. 12: 2; James 1: 5-6).

- We must take moral inventory of ourselves and admit when we are wrong (steps 4, 10; Lam. 3: 40; 1 Cor. 10: 12).

- We must make amends to those we have harmed, except when doing so will cause injury, and carry the message of deliverance to others (steps 8, 9, 12; Luke 6:31; Matt. 5: 23-24; Gal. 6: 1).

As is true with the *Roman Road to Recovery*, this program is based upon the assumption that an application of biblical truth over a period of time can bring about profound and lasting changes in the life of the abuser. It is of interest to note, however, that the steps outlined in this program are referred to as "steps of progress," emphasizing that progress, not perfection, is the goal of recovery.

While the AA model as well as the two preceding Christian adaptations of the model are designed, primarily, for use with the adult abuser, there is no reason why they cannot also be used with teenage abusers. If not in specific detail, certainly the basic features of such recovery programs can be adapted to meet their needs as well. For example, the following basic features of such programs readily lend themselves to teenage adaptation:

The desire to be cured: As is true with all such programs, teenagers must be willing to admit their helplessness in dealing with abuse and be motivated to seek help. This is the initial step in their recovery as it is with all self-help programs.

The use of the support-group principle: Teenagers would also profit by the opportunity to meet with peers on a regularly-scheduled basis for the purpose of sharing their struggles with abuse. They too need to recognize that they are not alone and that their problem is not unique.

The role of sponsorship: It would be tremendously helpful for the teenager to have someone in the peer group who would be a special friend and serve as a "lifeline" in case of emergency. Perhaps, even more realistically, an adult outside of the group, who is known and respected by the teenager, could serve such a critical role. While such an adult should not undermine the authority and responsibility of parents, a confidant outside of the family might serve a valuable non-judgmental role in helping a teenager gain insight and in providing support.

A biblical framework for recovery: Teenagers are as capable as adults of understanding and applying biblical principles to their recovery from abuse. More important than the specific biblical format is the consistency of applying principles that meet the needs of the teenagers. This is not the time for theologizing about great biblical truths; rather, it is the occasion for making practical biblical truths applicable and relevant to their struggle.

If you have teenagers who are drug abusers or if you know of someone who does, encourage them to seek out such a support group. More importantly, if your church does not have a program to help teenage abusers, speak to your Pastor and Youth Director and strongly urge them to see the need of such a ministry. Denying that the problem exists or ignoring the consequences of abuse is inexcusable for any church which claims the name of Christ and seeks to do His will. The church ought to be an important resource through which teenage abusers can seek help and support. Organizations such as "Overcomers Outreach" might be able to assist churches in developing such a program.[12]

In addition to the help received from such a support group, teenage abusers are, undoubtedly, going to need some form of "insight" therapy to further assist in the recovery process. For Christian teenagers, it is particularly critical that both the therapist and the philosophical basis of therapy reflect biblical principles.

The Uniqueness of Christian Treatment

The uniqueness of the Christian approach to treatment and recovery includes two very critical differences in contrast to secular approaches:

- the mindset and orientation of the therapist, and
- the breadth and completeness of the therapy process itself.

The mindset and orientation of Christian therapists is different from their secular counterparts in several different ways.

First of all, the presence of the Holy Spirit in their lives causes them to have a **spiritual wisdom** that is able to balance their secular knowledge and professional skills. We are told in I Cor. 2: 5-8 that Christian wisdom is different from worldly wisdom, and the therapist who knows Christ as his personal Savior will have such wisdom at his disposal.

Second, the minds of Christian therapists are open to an **understanding and interpretation** of many things (both spiritual and non-spiritual) that cannot be accessed by secular therapists. In II Cor. 4: 4, we are told that the god of this world blinds the mind of nonbelievers. There is no reason to believe that the minds of non-believing therapists are any less susceptible to such blindness than the average person.

Lastly, one has the right to expect the general orientation of Christian therapists to reflect **a different pattern** (strategy or approach) than their secular counterparts. In Rom. 12:2, we are instructed not to conform to the pattern of this world, and there is every reason to believe that such an admonition applies equally well to therapists as it does to the rest of us.

While it is most desirable for teenage drug abusers to seek out a Christian therapist, what should parents do if none is available in their immediate area? Depending upon how far the parents are willing or able to drive in order to seek such help, they may want to temporarily consider letting their teenager see a secular therapist. However, the parents should make sure that such a therapist is not antagonistic to a Christian view of life. Once these decisions have been made, don't delay in getting help for your teenager.

Of equal importance to the difference in mindset and orientation of Christian therapists is the difference in the breadth and completeness of the therapy process itself. Secular therapists tend to view the therapy process from a two-dimensional perspective—the physical and psychological needs of the patient. The problem with this narrow perspective is that it overlooks the spiritual nature of the individual and totally ignores the fact that many problems in the physical and psychological areas may have their roots in spiritual struggles.

In contrast, Christian therapy strives to meet the needs of the totally integrated individual—body, soul, and spirit. Anything less than such an approach denies the uniqueness of man (made in the image of God) and his ability to fellowship with God. We are told in I Thess. 5:23, that God desires that our *"whole spirit, soul, and body be kept blameless"* until Christ returns. It is the responsibility of every Christian therapist to address the spiritual needs of individuals as well as to demonstrate a concern for their physical and psychological needs.

Good therapy involves treatment in all three of these areas. The best alternative to drug abuse and the objective of all Christian therapy should be balanced living.[13] This means taking care of our **physical bodies** which, we have learned in a previous chapter, are temples of the living God. **For the soul**, this means gaining insight into our problem and ourselves and applying that insight to our growth and development. **For the spirit,** this means knowing the Lord personally, growing in our faith, and trusting Him for continued deliverance from our abuse. Anything less than such balanced living simply won't satisfy the needs of Christian teenagers or, for that matter, Christian adults.

Concluding Comments

In the final analysis, drug abuse must be recognized for what it is—sin, as well as physical and psychological bondage. It represents alienation from God as well as separation from one's physical health and psychological well-being. To view drug abuse as anything less ignores the human picture painted by Scripture and shortchanges the treatment/recovery process of Christian young people struggling with such a problem. The good news is that, as is true with any other sin, God's forgiveness is available to teenage drug abusers (I John 1: 9).

Successful drug treatment involves restoration with God and not simply physical and psychological healing. However, one should be careful not to confuse God's forgiveness with the assurance of immediate deliverance from the pattern of abuse. God can certainly deliver teenagers immediately from such bondage; however, deliverance more often involves a long, tedious process of struggle and prayer. The question is not whether God is able to deliver someone immediately from drug abuse but, rather, whether God chooses to do so. God's ways are not our ways (Isa. 55: 8) and we must be willing for Him to work out His will in the lives of our teenagers in His own time.

This is a hard lesson to learn, particularly when the lives of our young people are on the line. However, the fact remains that many teenagers may continue to struggle with the problem of drug abuse long after they have prayed the prayer of forgiveness. For them, the road to recovery may be long and treacherous. Furthermore, we have no right to assume that their continued struggle is an indication of their insincerity in desiring to get back on the spiritual track. Rather than be critical of their continued struggle, we should provide them with love and support, and pray that the power of Christ in their lives will finally enable them to conquer the problem.

As concerned Christian workers and parents, our primary responsibility is to make sure that Christian teenage drug abusers get proper help. This includes spiritual help as well as physical and psychological help. Anything less means we have failed our children. However, once we have done this, we must be willing to turn the problem over to the Lord and trust His guidance.

In Psalm 32: 8, God reminds us, *"I will instruct you and teach you in the way you should go; I will counsel you and watch over you"* (NIV). Do you believe His promise? May each of us experience God's presence in just such a personal way as we attempt to deal with the problems of drug abuse in the lives of our children.

Key questions answered by this chapter include:

1. What is the most reasonable goal of drug treatment?
2. What is the most recognized treatment program for chemical abuse?
3. How do the AA and medical-intervention models of treatment differ?
4. What are some examples of the Christian adaptation of theAA model?
5. Can principles of the AA model be used with teenage abusers?
6. What is unique about the orientation of the Christian therapist?
7. How does Christian therapy differ from secular therapy?
8. Does God's forgiveness assure immediate delivery from drug abuse?

Notes

Part Two

Drug Information

Chapter Ten

Prescription Drugs

Prescription drugs are drugs dispensed to the consumer only with the written approval of a licensed medical practitioner—a physician or, in some instances, a dentist. The economics of prescription drugs is unique in that a second party—a physician—dictates what the consumer (patient) will purchase. Thus, the promotion of drugs is directed at the physician, not the patient.

In general, prescription drugs are more potent and have greater potential for producing undesirable side effects, thus requiring close supervision by a physician. Such drugs can only be purchased through a pharmacy, and it is the responsibility of the pharmacist to see that the physician's instructions (usually written in Latin) are accurately translated and passed on to the consumer in a language they understand. Although physicians are able to prescribe a wide range of drug types, they are bound by certain legal requirements. For example, no drugs in the Federal Government's Schedule I (see Appendix B) may be prescribed for medical use.[1]

While the prescription is written in a kind of shorthand easily understood by physicians and pharmacists, the consumer would do well to learn the basic features of prescription writing. Although the exact meaning of the all-too-familiar symbol "Rx" is somewhat obscure, most sources state that it stands for the Latin "take thou" or for the Latin word meaning "recipe".[2] In either case, the instructional nature of the prescription is made clear.

All prescriptions, by law, are required to contain specific instructions to the pharmacist on how to dispense the drug and instructions to the consumer on how to take the drug. In the latter case, instructions on the medication container label tell the patient how many pills to take, when they should be taken and any additional instructions that might be required. The name of the drug is typically written in its brand (trade) form or as a generic substitute, if available. Since current law also dictates how often various drugs can be refilled, this information is also provided in the lower left-hand corner of the prescription and passed on to the patient. Finally, the physician's signature, address and drug certification number are included in the lower right-hand corner of the prescription. The certification number authorizes the physician to prescribe drugs and is assigned by the Drug Enforcement Administration of the Federal Government. As for the illegibility of most physicians' signatures, pharmacists, fortunately, tend to be as good at deciphering cryptic writing as they are at translating Latin instructions.

Most prescription drugs available today are designed to treat specific mental or physical symptoms. Some prescription drugs are designed to treat specific psychiatric disorders, while others are designed to serve a broader psychotherapeutic role in cases where psychiatric disorders are not apparent. Still other prescription drugs are designed to treat specific physical symptoms with little or no attention given to the psychological characteristics of the disorder. In the following sections, each of these categories of prescription drugs will be considered along with specific examples of drugs that represent the categories. For the sake of consistency and practicality, brand names of drugs will be used. In those few instances where the author deviates from this policy, the drug is probably better known by its generic name than by its brand name.

Psychiatric Drugs

Psychiatric drugs are prescription drugs used in the treatment of such psychiatric disorders as anxiety, depression and the severe psychotic condition called schizophrenia. While it is not the intent of this chapter to go into great detail on the nature of these psychiatric disorders, each is clearly defined by a set of specific symptoms.[3] Furthermore, such information is readily available to physicians (usually psychiatrists) who prescribe drugs for such treatment.

Antianxiety drugs (also referred to as anxiolytics or minor tranquilizers) are used to treat anxiety—that vague uncomfortable or apprehensive feeling we have when things are not going well. In some instances, anxiety can be tied to a specific event or person; however, in other instances, it has an undefined source and is called "free floating" anxiety. Antianxiety drugs reverse the symptoms of anxiety and produce a general quieting effect on the central nervous system.

The first of these drugs to be marketed was Miltown which served primarily as a muscle relaxant. However, most antianxiety drugs used today belong to a class referred to as benzodiazepines. Three of the most popular antianxiety drugs belonging to this class are Librium, Valium and Xanax. As will be indicated in a later section, some benzodiazepines are also useful as sleeping aids.

Antidepressant drugs are used to treat the very serious condition of depression—a mood disturbance in which one feels "down in spirit" and dejected. While everyone may on occasion feel depressed, some people experience a prolonged debilitation by such a mood change and require medication. Antidepressant drugs reverse the depression experienced in these more severe instances and return the person to a more normal mood.

Most of the antidepressant drugs available today are either MAO (monoamine oxidase) inhibitors or tricyclic antidepressants. Two of the most popular antidepressant drugs on the market today are Nardil and Tofranil. However, a new generation of antidepressant drugs is represented by the drug Prozac. While Prozac has gained a reputation for producing adverse reactions (including thoughts of suicide), it probably is as effective and no more dangerous than any of the antidepressant drugs. In those cases where depression is accompanied by mania (a hyper-aroused state) the treatment drug of choice is Lithium. This drug helps to stabilize the mood, preventing it from swinging in either direction.

Antipsychotic drugs (also referred to as neuroleptic drugs or major tranquilizers) are used to treat a form of psychosis known as schizophrenia—a severe disorganization of personality, thought and emotion. Such a condition is also frequently accompanied by hallucinations (false perceptions) and delusions (false beliefs). Prior to the advent of these drugs, patients diagnosed as having schizophrenia had to be confined to the psychiatric wards of our nation's hospitals.[4] However, with these drugs, most patients can be treated on an out-patient basis and live at home under supervision.

Most of the antipsychotic drugs available today belong to either the phenothiazine or butyrophenone class. Three of the most popular antipsychotic drugs available today are Thorazine, Stelazine, and Haldol. One of the long-term problems associated with the use of these antipsychotic drugs is the occurrence of movement disturbances (twitches and tremors). However, a newer type of antipsychotic drug, Clozaril, appears to effectively treat symptoms of schizophrenia without producing such undesirable side effects.

Psychiatric drugs have revolutionized the treatment of mental disorders and enabled many patients to be free of the debilitating symptoms accompanying such disorders. However, it is important to keep in mind that psychiatric drugs do not cure the mental disorder for which they are prescribed. When drug treatment is withheld, the symptoms of the mental disorder reoccur. Therefore, the benefit of psychiatric drugs is one of management, not cure.

Psychotherapeutic Drugs

While the distinction between psychiatric drugs and psychotherapeutic drugs is somewhat arbitrary, the latter category refers primarily to drugs used in the clinical treatment of conditions where no specific psychiatric disorders are present.

Stimulants are used clinically to treat several behavioral disorders, the most prevalent being childhood Attention Deficit Hyperactivity Disorder (ADHD).[5] This behavioral problem is more commonly known as "hyperactivity" and is characterized by attention problems, distractability, impulsive actions and, of course, hyperactivity. While, in some cases, the problem seems to be reduced once the child (usually a boy) reaches puberty, many hyperactive children continue to have antisocial problems in adulthood. Hyperactive children have difficulty performing in the highly structured environment of a classroom and usually are put in a special class environment where they can receive the individual attention they need. Stimulant drugs reduce the symptoms of hyperactivity and have a general "normalizing" effect on the behavior of the child. Since stimulant drugs normally increase activity, not decrease it, this "normalizing" effect on hyperactive children is called a "paradoxical" one.

Although amphetamine has been used to treat hyperactive children, Ritalin is the drug of choice by most physicians. While amphetamine and Ritalin are very similar in their structure and action, a different type of stimulant, Cylert, has also been used with some success in the treatment of hyperactivity. Stimulant drugs are also used to treat conditions of fatigue and narcolepsy (uncontrollable episodes of falling asleep during the daytime), as well as serving as an aid to weight loss. Amphetamine, in particular, has appetite-suppressing (anorexic) effects and may help in a short-term program of weight reduction.

Sedative-hypnotic drugs are used, in small doses, to produce sedation (relaxed state) and, in larger doses, to induce sleep. Prior to the advent of antianxiety drugs, sedative-hypnotics were prescribed for the treatment of anxiety. However, sedative-hypnotics are more potent and have a smaller margin of safety (see Appendix A) than do antianxiety drugs. Thus, they are seldom used today for the treatment of anxiety and related problems.

Sedative-hypnotics are, however, still valuable in preparing patients for surgery and in serving as general anesthetics.

The means by which sedative hypnotics bring about their effects appears to be similar to that of the antianxiety drugs. Most of the sedative-hypnotics in use today belong to a class known as barbiturates. This class of drugs has been in medical use for over 80 years and includes specific examples of drugs which differ, primarily, in the duration of their action.[6] That is to say, some barbiturates are short-acting, others intermediate-acting and still others long-acting. Three of the standard barbiturates available today are Seconal, Amytal and Luminal. Luminal is a long-acting barbiturate and has a duration of action from 6 to 10 hours.

While larger doses of barbiturates can be used to induce sleep, certain antianxiety drugs have increasingly replaced them in the sleeping-pill market. In the late 1980's, the antianxiety drug Halcion became the most commonly prescribed sleeping pill. Although this drug has been accused of inciting bizarre and antisocial behavior, it, along with another antianxiety drug (Dalmane), continue to be widely prescribed as sleep aids. Since sleeping pills differ in their duration of action as do barbiturates, one might be preferred over the other on the basis of the need to merely initiate sleep or to sustain it for most of the night.

Analgesic narcotics are drugs used in the clinical treatment of pain, whatever its source and nature. The word analgesic means the blocking of pain without causing unconsciousness and the word narcotic means that the drugs are derivatives of the opium poppy. While the potential medicinal value of the opium poppy has probably been known since biblical times (see Chapter 3), it is only recently that researchers have discovered how opioids block pain. It appears that opioids block pain by facilitating the release of certain brain chemicals which, in turn, block the pathways carrying the sensation of pain.

The two most commonly prescribed opioid drugs are morphine and codeine. While both of these drugs are natural ingredients of the opium poppy, they are synthesized in the laboratory for medical use. A common strategy for the prescribing of opioids is to combine them with an over-the-counter (OTC) analgesic. For example, one of the top 25 prescription medications in use today is Tylenol with codeine.[7] While Tylenol use does not require a prescription, combining it with codeine brings the medication under prescription control.

Additional synthetic drugs that are designed to copy the activity of natural opioids include Demerol and Darvon. Attempts to chemically alter the structure of morphine has also resulted in the drug heroin. While heroin is classified as a Schedule I drug and, thus, is not prescribed for the clinical treatment of pain, it has caused social havoc as an illicit drug. We will have more to say about that in Chapter 12.

Finally, it is important to note that the potential for abusing and developing a dependency on opioid drugs is very high. In fact, one might say that opioids are the drug class "par excellence" for abuse and dependency. The reason for this appears to be, not only their pain relieving properties, but their ability to produce a euphoric effect (a heightened sense of psychological well-being). Such effects are extremely reinforcing and create a strong "craving" for such drugs. As a general rule, it is important that such drugs be prescribed with restraint and for the shortest possible duration. Because of their high potential for abuse and dependency, it is also critical that we teach our young people to avoid their use for any reason other than a properly supervised treatment of pain by a physician.

Additional Prescription Drugs

While covering every possible type of prescription drugs is beyond the scope of this chapter, the author does want to mention three additional types of medication. These types are quite diverse in their use and action but do share the common characteristics of being among the most popular prescription medications.[8]

Antihypertensive (high blood pressure) drugs enjoy a prescription popularity rivaled only by anxiety drugs. I suppose one should not be surprised to find that both antihypertensive and antianxiety drugs have a beneficial role to play in our competitive and highly stressful society. Cardiovascular problems are widespread among the middle-aged and elderly, and people are living much longer than in previous years. Both of these factors increase the risk of developing high blood pressure as well as other symptoms of stress.

Antihypertensive medication can, in most instances, control blood pressure adequately, but such medication does not remove the source of the problem. Antihypertensive medications work by different means, with three of the most popular types being diuretics (increasing urine production), calcium channel blockers (blocking calcium passage across cell membranes), and ACE inhibitors (inhibiting formation of a hypertensive chemical).

Examples of these types of drugs include Dyazide, Calan and Zestril, respectively. While hypertensive patients are usually started out on a diuretic, it frequently requires the addition of another drug for the effective control of blood pressure. It is also important to recognize that what works for one hypertensive patient may not be sufficient for another patient. Finding the right medication and the right dose to control the blood pressure of a particular patient is very much a "trial and error" process. This is not so much the fault of the physician as it is due to the complex causes of hypertension.

Most cases of high blood pressure are defined as "essential hypertension", meaning the causes are multiple and differ from person to person. Thus, patients might be expected to react differently to different medications. Most antihypertensive medications have undesirable side effects (dizziness, etc.) and it becomes a major problem to convince patients to continue on their medication.

Antiulcer drugs enjoy a prescription popularity for many of the same reasons that antihypertensive and antianxiety drugs do.

Not only does stress increase the likelihood of hypertension, but it also markedly increases the likelihood of ulcers forming in the digestive tract. In the most severe cases, such ulcers can erupt and cause bleeding. Hopefully, the problem would be identified and treated before reaching this stage. It is of interest to note that ulcers are not caused by stress *per se*, but by the reaction of the body following stress.[9] It is during the period following stress that stomach acid levels increase, literally eating away the walls of the stomach.

The most popular antiulcer medication in use today is Zantac. This drug counteracts the action of stomach acid and protects the wall of the digestive system from being damaged. It is also quite obvious that a patient feels much better after a reduction in stomach acid, explaining the often claimed general benefits of the drug. Recently, a non-prescription form of Zantac (Zantac 75) has become available as an OTC medication. Such increased availability will undoubtedly further increase the popularity of the drug.

Oral contraceptives comprise a final type of prescription drug that will be mentioned in this section. While even ten years ago, oral contraceptives would most likely not have been listed among the top 40 most prescribed medications, the so-called "sexual revolution" has given them this ignoble distinction of popularity. Rather than dealing with the underlying problem of sexual morality, society has chosen the route of so-called "safe sex".

While no preventive measure is foolproof, the increased popularity of oral contraceptives among young adults is a vivid reminder of where society is heading and its willingness to play the "safe sex" game. Hopefully, Christian young people will not be caught up in such a "no-win" game. On the more positive side, oral contraceptives do, of course, have a legitimate role in the family planning of married couples, including Christian families.

The oral contraceptives on the market today are a combination of two female hormones and work by way of interrupting the ovarian cycle.[10] One example of this type of medication is Ortho-Novum.

Conclusion

Prescription drugs are big business when you consider the fact that approximately 1.6 billion medicines are prescribed annually in this country. Of this number, nearly 800 million are new prescriptions and over 700 million are refills.[11]

With such an abundance of prescription drugs on the market, it should not surprise anyone to learn that they are widely abused. We normally think of abused drugs as being illegal (illicit) drugs; however, the widespread availability of prescription drugs also makes them a strong candidate for abuse. Remember, prescription drugs are potent in their action and frequently have dangerous side effects. Thus, the unauthorized use ... or over use of prescription medication can be just as dangerous as is the use of illegal drugs.

While a few physicians are all too willing to prescribe powerful medications with potentially dangerous side effects, most instances of abuse are due to illegal or irresponsible actions on the part of the consumer. For example, chronic drug abusers (including young abusers) are quite happy to get their hands on prescription drugs rather than on illicit street drugs. Prescription drugs are not only more potent in their effect, but protect the abuser from many of the dangers of "street drug" contamination.

On the other hand, some drug abuse may be the result of unsupervised, irresponsible action. Some patients may increase their supply of a particular medication by getting prescriptions from several physicians, or elderly persons may end up taking more of a drug than they should out of ignorance or confusion. Fortunately, most pharmacies keep a cross-check on a patient's medication and are able to reduce the likelihood of such occurrences.

Contrary to the rampant prescription practices of many physicians, some physicians' fear of drugs causes them to indulge in what one author calls "psychiatric Calvinism".[12] They are reluctant to use certain drugs and, instead, encourage patients to "tough it out". In some cases, there is a reluctance to use certain drugs, although they may be the best treatment available. If for example, a physician is reluctant to prescribe a "pain killer" for a terminal cancer patient because of the fear of addiction, it would appear that medical priorities are distorted. While restraint in the prescribing of drugs is a noble policy, such a policy should not include depriving patients of needed medication.

Prescription drugs are both a curse and a blessing. They are a curse in the sense that our society will probably never get a handle on their potential for abuse any more than it is able to get a handle on illegal drug abuse. They are a blessing in that, with properly supervised use, they improve the quality of life for all of us, Christian and non-Christian, alike. As for Christians specifically, prescription drugs can play a valuable role in sustaining our health and facilitating our ministry for the cause of Christ. Furthermore, it is our duty as Christian adults to teach our young people a proper respect for prescription drugs and how to make sound decisions regarding their legitimate use. Let's not fail in this critical task.

Key questions answered by this chapter include:

1. What are prescription drugs?
2. What information is required on a written prescription?
3. What psychiatric disorders are treated with prescription drugs?
4. How do psychotherapeutic and psychiatric drugs differ?
5. How do stimulant drugs help hyperactive children?
6. What are the most popular prescription medications?
7. How are prescription drugs both a "curse" and a "blessing"?
8. Is there a serious danger of abusing prescription drugs?

Notes

Chapter Eleven

Over-The-Counter (OTC) Drugs

Have you ever had a bad cold or a severe headache? Of course you have, who hasn't? Then you know what it is like to walk the aisles of your local drugstore and be confronted with the bewildering array of medicines available to you without prescriptions. The sheer volume of available medicines is enough to totally confuse you, to say nothing of trying to decide which one is best for you and your family.

Welcome to the world of OTC drugs. It is a highly competitive world with different drug companies jockeying for top position and trying to convince you that their product is the best. So fierce is the competition that Americans spend more than $7 billion annually on such drugs.[1] As large as this figure might be, it still is less than Americans spend on prescription drugs, alcohol or cigarettes.

OTC drugs are unique in the sense that they represent a class of drugs that are self-prescribed for the treatment of a self-diagnosed illness. Very seldom is a physician or other health professional consulted in the process of treatment. While such self-administered treatment has its advantages in terms of saving time and perhaps money, it also places an increased responsibility on the individual to make sound choices. OTC drugs are usually less potent and dangerous than prescription drugs; however, they are still drugs and must be treated with caution and respect. Fortunately, the FDA regulates the safety and effectiveness of OTC medication as it does prescription drugs.[2] This allows consumers to focus on more practical matters such as matching the ingredients of a drug with their particular symptoms.

The purpose of this chapter is two-fold:

- to discuss the most common types of OTC medications available to the public; and
- to present some practical guidelines that should help you sort through the array of OTC medicines and make wise choices in the selection of a particular drug.

The first of these objectives is no small task, considering the fact that there are 26 different categories of OTC drugs;[3] however, we will look at only four of these that appear to be most prevalent in the consumer's eye—Diet Aids, Sleeping Aids, Analgesics (pain killers) and Cold Remedies. The second of these objectives, while involving some information not readily available to the consumer, also involves some "common-sense" suggestions that we all need to follow.

Diet Aids

Prior to the Substance Control Act of 1970, the consumer was able to purchase OTC diet pills containing the powerful appetite-suppressant/stimulant, amphetamine. This is no longer the case. Most of the weight-control products on the market today contain the stimulant phenlypropanolamine (PPA). The FDA considers PPA to be a safe and effective appetite suppressant although there is some question about the long-term effectiveness of the drug.[4] Caffeine appears to increase the effectiveness of PPA and, for a while, was combined with PPA in OTC appetite suppressants.[5] However, concern about the safety of combining the two substances led to a reversal of this policy and, presently, diet aids contain only PPA.

Parenthetically, while caffeine is a much milder stimulant than PPA, it may have some appetite-suppressant effects on its own and should not be overlooked for its potential role as a diet aid. Thus, your morning coffee and subsequent coffee breaks may do more than simply keep you going throughout the day. Nor do non-coffee drinkers need to lose heart, for tea and most soft drinks contain significant amounts of caffeine as well.

It is of interest to note that most of the competing weight-control products on the market today are essentially the same—they all contain PPA as the active ingredient. Furthermore, many of these different products are made by the same company. This is the case with two of the most popular weight-control products—Control and Dexatrim.[6] Such multiple packaging of roughly the same product is obviously designed to cover the market and serves only to further confuse the consumer. Different names of products do not, in any way, assure the consumer that they are getting different medicines. There are presently no laws against the practice of multiple packaging of the same product and consumers need to be alerted to such duplication.

While the FDA routinely reviews additional OTC weight-control products, none are presently available. Furthermore, even with the availability of products containing PPA, the best diet program may still be common sense—a balanced diet coupled with a good exercise program. Let's also teach our young people good weight control practices and discourage them from depending upon pills to do the job. Of course, there may be exceptions to this simple rule, particularly in those instances where weight problems may have a genetic basis.[7]

Sleep Aids

OTC sleep aids are designed to produce a mild sedative or calming effect, thereby facilitating the onset of sleep. They do not, as is commonly assumed, literally put one to sleep as is the case with more powerful prescription drugs called "sedative-hypnotics". Most of the sleep aids available on the market today contain antihistamines (either pyrilamine maleate or diphen-hydramine). While antihistamines are typically used in the treatment of allergic reactions, they also have the additional side-effect of producing drowsiness. It is this side-effect property of drowsiness that is basic to the effectiveness of sleep aids. Two examples of such sleep aids are Sominex and Sleep-Eze.

While the general problem of insomnia may be somewhat overstated, there are obviously people (both young and old) who have difficulty in falling asleep. In those instances, sleep aids may be helpful and should be taken at least 20-30 minutes before retiring. Since the effects of antihistamines are enhanced by the action of alcohol, one needs to be very cautious about combining such medication with alcoholic beverages before retiring. Our young people in particular, need to be reminded of the dangers of such practices.

Some time-honored remedies may also prove to be effective in combating insomnia including a glass of warm milk before retiring.[8] Milk, particularly when it is warmed, contains significant amounts of L-tryptophan, a chemical necessary to the brain's regulation of sleep. Furthermore, carbohydrates facilitate the absorption of L-tryptophan. So go ahead, have your glass of warm milk and cookies before going to bed. You may find that it helps you fall asleep. In any event, it will not hurt.

Analgesics

Analgesics (literally meaning without pain) comprise a large group of OTC drugs used to treat pain. While there is, again, a large number of such "pain killers" on the open market, the number of active ingredients involved in such products is quite small. With few exceptions, the active ingredients are acetylsalicylic acid, acetaminophen or ibuprofen. An example of each of these categories of active ingredients will be briefly discussed, along with some attempt to consider both the benefits and risks of such products.

Aspirin (acetylsalicylic acid) is, without a doubt, the oldest and most time-honored analgesic on the market today. Aspirin is not only an extremely effective analgesic (blocking pain in the mild to moderate range), but has additional clinical benefits as well. For one, it is extremely effective in reducing body temperature when it is elevated by fever (antipyretic action). Fortunately, it does not reduce body temperature in the absence of fever and, thus, can be safely used to treat conditions not accompanied by an increase in temperature. Secondly, aspirin is an effective anti-inflammatory agent; i.e., it is effective in reducing inflammation and soreness in joints or injured areas of the body. It is this action that makes the drug a favorite choice in the treatment of arthritis.

However, aspirin is not without its problems and has some potentially serious side effects. It can cause stomach irritation (and even bleeding) and should be avoided by persons having stomach problems. Buffered preparations of the drug may help to counteract this effect. Aspirin can also block the coagulation of blood and can prolong bleeding in some instances. While this effect is a clear disadvantage in one sense, it may be very useful in preventing a stroke and heart attack. In fact, many health professionals swear by its effectiveness as a preventive measure. On balance, aspirin, when taken as recommended and with caution, is a valuable drug and deserving of its wide acceptance.

Tylenol (acetaminophen) is a competitor of aspirin and, as a result of aggressive advertising in the 1970's, has found its way into the bigtime. As is true with aspirin, Tylenol is an effective analgesic and, in some instances, may be the product of choice. If only relief from pain and fever reduction is desired, Tylenol may be preferred over aspirin, since it does not typically irritate the stomach as does aspirin. However, Tylenol is not an effective anti-inflammatory agent and, thus, should not be used in the treatment of arthritis or soreness of joints. Many people, unknowingly, take the drug for such a purpose and expose themselves to unnecessary risk of overdosing on the drug. In fact, the most serious side effect of Tylenol is that associated with overdosing. In such a case, the toxic effects of Tylenol are probably more serious than those of aspirin and may result in liver and possibly kidney damage. Thus, Tylenol is not necessarily safer than aspirin but, when taken as prescribed, may be an effective alternative to aspirin.

Advil (ibuprofen) is another type of analgesic which is rapidly gaining in popularity. While it shares its "pain killing" effectiveness with both aspirin and Tylenol, it has other unique properties of its own. Unlike aspirin and Tylenol, Advil is not very effective in reducing body temperature associated with a fever. However, the drug has a powerful anti-inflammatory action, which often may make it the drug of choice in the treatment of arthritis. Furthermore, its use as a drug (whether for its analgesic effects or anti-inflammatory action) may be more effective than aspirin, without the accompanying side effects of the latter. Advil is not, however, without side effects and in some instances can cause nausea, stomach pain and cramping.

While **Motrin** (also containing ibuprofen) was previously a prescription drug, it is now available as an OTC product.

Aleve (naproxen) and **Orudis** (ketoprofen) are two relatively new arrivals to the analgesic pool of OTC drugs. Both appear to be effective in the treatment of pain and have anti-inflammatory action. However, their general usefulness in comparison to the traditional analgesics awaits the test of time. Since pain is often pervasive, and varies in intensity from mild to excruciating, it is no wonder OTC analgesics enjoy such a wide popularity. However, we should exercise caution in their use and encourage our young people to do the same.

Cold Remedies

While there is presently no known cure for the cold, it is possible to treat the symptoms of a cold while it is running its natural course. It is in this context that cold remedies play a valuable role. Since cold symptoms tend to be quite complex, cold remedies usually include several active ingredients, each designed to treat a particular symptom.

While there are exceptions to the rule, the common types of ingredients found in most cold remedies include the following:[9]

- Antihistamines (chlorpheniramine maleate or diphenhydramine) for the relief of sneezing and runny nose.
- Decongestants (pseudoephedrine or PPA) for the relief of swollen membranes in the nasal passages.
- Analgesics/antipyretics (aspirin or acetaminophen) for the relief of aches and to reduce body temperature associated with fever.
- Antitussive (dextromethorphan) for the relief and suppression of cough.

Various common cold remedies contain different combinations of the above active ingredients. For example, the popular Tylenol Cold medication contains all four of the above categories of ingredients. However, the equally popular Contac (12-hour) contains only an antihistamine and a decongestant. Contac may not, therefore, be the best choice if your congestion is accompanied by aches and pains and severe coughing. While Contac is marketed as an effective cold remedy, it is probably more similar to allergy and sinus medications than to other cold remedies. An allergy medication such as Allerest also contains only an antihistamine and a decongestant. However, a sinus medication such as Sinutab contains an analgesic as well as an antihistamine and a decongestant, probably because of the pain and discomfort associated with sinus problems.

When the primary discomfort associated with a cold is congestion, it may be helpful to use a decongestant in the form of a nasal spray. For example, Neo-Synephrine (12 hour) contains a powerful and long lasting decongestant and is quite effective in treating the discomfort associated with congestion.[10] Furthermore, this particular decongestant, because it only needs to be taken every 12 hours, has a relatively low risk associated with its use. However, if someone takes such a nasal spray over an extended period of time, there is a serious risk of a rebound of nasal congestion and stuffiness upon termination of the medication. Therefore, one must be cautious about the use of such nasal sprays and, in particular, avoid combining them with other cold medications which contain a decongestant. Since decongestants have powerful stimulant properties, they are frequently abused by young people; therefore, we need to be on the alert for such practices.

Additional OTC Medications

While the primary focus of this chapter is on the preceding four categories of OTC drugs, brief mention will be made of a few additional types of medication that also enjoy a high degree of use as personal remedies for a variety of problems. For example, **antacids** (Alka-Seltzer, Maalox, Mylanta) are widely used for the temporary relief of acid indigestion. Such medication should, however, be taken only on a temporary basis, for the underlying symptoms may be due to a more serious condition; e.g., an ulcer.

Antidiarrheals (Pepto-Bismol, Kaopectate) which are designed to treat diarrhea and **laxatives** (Ex-Lax, Correctol) which are designed to treat constipation are also popular personal remedies. However, if symptoms of diarrhea or constipation persist, they too, could be indicative of a more serious underlying condition needing medical attention.

Finally, **vitamins** (One-a-Day and similar preparations) enjoy a high degree of popularity as an OTC product and are used for the treatment of every possible condition ranging from the common cold to cancer. While vitamins can, when taken in proper amounts be a valuable supplement to the daily diet, taking more vitamins than is needed can also be harmful. Like all OTC preparations, they are drugs and should be treated with the same respect and caution rendered all drugs.

Guidelines for Choosing an OTC Drug

Do you feel any better about walking down the aisle of your local drug store and being confronted by the array of OTC medications than you did at the beginning of this chapter? Probably not, yet. However, hang on, for this section of the chapter is specifically designed to give you some practical guidelines for plowing through the bewildering world of OTC drugs. It is hoped that the following guidelines will not only put you at ease in choosing an OTC product but, also, give you a sound basis for making such a choice.

- Read the ingredients on the label, not simply the product name.

While there are many different product names on the market, most of the OTC medications can be reduced to seven basic ingredients.[11] These ingredients include: two analgesics (aspirin, acetaminophen), two antihistamines (chlorpheniramine maleate, diphenhydramine), two stimulant decongestants (PPA, pseudo-ephedrine) and one cough suppressant (dextromethorphan).

Two or more products with different names may contain exactly the same ingredients, and there is no particular reason to prefer one over the other unless you can save a little money in doing so. Don't let the popularizing of certain products by television or other media dupe you into believing it is different (or better), unless you have demonstrated to your own satisfaction that the ingredients are different. A careful reading of the ingredients is the "rule of thumb" and the secret to de-mystifying the world of OTC products.

- Treat only the symptoms you have, not those you don't have.

We have all heard the expression, "If it isn't broken, don't fix it." Well, the expression applies equally well to the choice of an OTC product. If you don't have a particular symptom, don't buy a product that treats it. Or putting it another way, if you don't need a particular ingredient, don't use it. Such a guideline becomes particularly critical in the choice of multiple-ingredient products like cold remedies. If you have only a limited number of cold-related symptoms, choose a remedy that is designed to treat only those symptoms. Of couse, this again requires that you read the list of ingredients carefully and attempt to match symptoms with ingredients.

- Buy the generic form of OTC medications, whenever available.

Many of the larger drugstore chains are coming out with their own generic form of single and multiple-ingredient products. This is particularly true in the case of analgesics and cold remedies. You can usually buy acetaminophen or ibuprofen by name, and these are exactly the same analgesics that are found in the more popular brands like Tylenol and Advil.

Cold remedies of the drugstore generic form also include the exact same ingredients that you find in the more popular cold and allergy products like Tylenol-Cold, Allerest and Sinutab. More importantly, a significant savings can be realized by choosing the generic form of a particular OTC drug, since the cost of brand-name products is greatly inflated.[12]

- Avoid the use of OTC drugs in combination with prescription drugs, whenever possible.

While OTC drugs are less potent and less dangerous than prescription drugs, they are, nevertheless, drugs. Therefore, one has to be extremely careful about the choice and use of OTC products when you are taking prescribed medication for some condition.

One of the commonly reported side effects of blood-pressure medication (a prescription drug) is that of drowsiness. Combining such a medication with an OTC product containing antihistamine action could further increase the drowsiness and be a potential danger. Also, combining such a medication with an OTC product containing stimulant decongestants could have the opposite effect, thereby reducing the effectiveness of the blood-pressure medication. Don't take any chances in combining OTC products with prescribed medication, particularly with children. If it becomes necessary to do so, get professional advice on such potential dangers.

- If in doubt, ask the pharmacist.

Pharmacists are trained professionals who are knowledgeable about OTC products as well as prescription drugs. Therefore, don't hesitate to ask them for advice or an explanation in regard to the choice of an OTC product. Pharmacists also have at their disposal valuable information about the interaction of different drugs (OTC and prescription) and will gladly provide you with such information upon request. Don't hesitate to take advantage of their presence and knowledge.

Now, let's take a walk down the aisle where the OTC products are displayed and see how much you have learned. Hopefully, it is not quite as frightening as before, and you feel a little more comfortable in choosing an OTC product. More importantly, take a young person with you the next time you walk down the aisle where the OTC products are located and pass on to them what you have learned from these suggested guidelines.

Key questions answered by this chapter:

1. How do OTC drugs differ from prescription drugs?
2. What are the most common types of OTC medications?
3. Do OTC diet aids have long-term effectiveness?
4. Do OTC sleep aids really put you to sleep?
5. What are the benefits of different OTC "pain killers"?
6. What are the active ingredients of common OTC cold remedies?
7. What are some guidelines for choosing an OTC drug?

Notes

Chapter Twelve

Illicit (illegal) Drugs

Up to this point, we have considered what are commonly known as "legal drugs". Such a label applies to prescription drugs and OTC drugs which were discussed in the preceding two chapters. The present chapter focuses on what are commonly known as "illicit" or illegal drugs. These drugs, with rare exceptions, are not manufactured, distributed or sold legally. Furthermore, illicit drugs have two additional characteristics which distinguish them from most legal drugs.

First, many illicit drugs are imported from foreign countries. For example, almost one-half of all the heroin sold in the U. S. is imported from Mexico and the bulk of the cocaine sold on our streets is imported from Peru and Columbia.[1] Because of the uncertainty of these sources, there is no way of judging the quality or purity of such products.

Second, those illicit drugs that are not imported illegally are produced by small clandestine laboratories in the U. S. These laboratories are usually fairly mobile (can be moved quickly) and relatively crude (may be set up in a kitchen, basement or garage). Since most of the individuals working in these laboratories are not professionals and, thus, have limited chemical skills, there is the potential for chemical error as well as contamination by impurities. Because of the lack of standards with illicit drugs (which are present with legal drugs), the abuser stands a much higher risk with their use. Indeed, this risk can be life-threatening, and there is reason to believe that many deaths associated with illicit drug abuse are due to miscalculation of doses and adulterants contained in the product, not to the drug itself.

With these potential hazards in mind, the purpose of the present chapter is:

- to briefly discuss the basic characteristics of abuse patterns associated with illicit drugs, and
- to discuss some common types of illicit drugs.

Regarding the latter objective, no attempt will be made to cover exhaustively all illicit drugs; rather, the discussion will be limited to those that are most commonly abused and for which there is the greatest concern by Christian workers and parents of teenagers.

Abuse Patterns Associated with Illicit Drugs

While the frequency and characterization of drug abuse might be described in a number of different ways, the patterns outlined by Siegel[2] are particularly helpful in understanding the nature of drug abuse among young people. These patterns include: experimental, social-recreational, circumstantial-situational, intensified and compulsive. Each of these will be briefly considered in order to show that abuse takes many forms as well as differing in the degree of involvement.

Experimental: This pattern of abuse is defined as short-term experimenting with drugs and has a limited frequency of occurrence (perhaps no more than half a dozen times). Such abuse is largely motivated by curiosity or pressure by one's peers to try the drug. While such experimenting with drugs is not harmless, it is a relatively low-level form of abuse compared to other patterns discussed.

Social-recreational: This is, perhaps, the most common pattern of abuse observed among young people and is characterized by the sharing of the drug experience with friends or acquaintances. Typically, the drug is seen by the abusers as a "social lubricant" and is taken for the purpose of facilitating social interaction and function. This form of abuse is more frequent than the experimental pattern and, while social pressures within the group tend to regulate the use of the drug, the risks associated with this form of abuse are considerable.

Circumstantial-situational: This pattern is defined by the abuse of drugs under certain specific circumstances or in certain specific situations for the purpose of enhancing mood or performance. For example, a young person may abuse drugs at a rock concert for the purpose of enhancing the excitement associated with the event. In the same manner, a young person may abuse drugs to get over a broken relationship or the death of a close friend. This pattern of abuse may be more or less frequent than the social-recreational pattern and also carries with it a high degree of risk.

Intensified: This pattern is described as a long-term use of drugs at least once a day and is motivated by the desire to achieve and maintain some level of performance or relief on a relatively permanent basis. For example, a teenager may smoke marijuana daily in order to be accepted by his circle of close friends, never realizing that he is living his life in a constant "drug state". Teenagers who take drugs daily in order to counteract chronic depression would also fit this pattern of abuse. This pattern of abuse is more serious than any of the preceding ones and is characterized by the person who is "hooked" on drugs. The risks associated with such a pattern can be staggering and life-threatening.

Compulsive: This pattern is characterized by a high frequency and high intensity of drug abuse over a long duration. The individual is preoccupied with drugs and drug-seeking behavior, and his whole life is centered around such activity to the exclusion of other normal social behaviors. He is totally dependent on the drug and would experience serious physical and psychological discomfort with its withdrawal. Since withdrawal can be life-threatening, the person continues with the abuse pattern in order to avoid such a risk. This pattern of abuse is the most serious of all and, essentially, describes an individual who is unable to function properly in society. Hopefully, teenagers can be helped before reaching this stage of abuse.

In general, the above patterns of abuse progress from a simple curiosity with drugs to a preoccupation with drugs. Thus, abuse comes in all forms and shapes. While we may be quite willing to accept the fact that the intensified and compulsive patterns are clear instances of abuse, we may be more reticent to accept experimental, social-recreational and circumstantial-situational patterns as such. However, one could argue that all forms of illegal drug use might be defined as abuse and that even such limited involvement with drugs stands the risk of becoming intensified or compulsive. There is, therefore, nothing to be gained by referring only to the last two patterns as abuse. Realizing that drug abuse takes many forms, let us now look at some specific types of illicit drugs that are widely abused.

Commonly Abused Illicit Drugs

The most commonly abused illicit drugs include: stimulants, opiates, hallucinogens, marijuana and anabolic steroids. Each of these types will be briefly discussed, with the discussion focusing primarily on the potential danger associated with their abuse.

Stimulants: The most commonly abused stimulants are amphetamine (speed) and cocaine (coke). Both of these drugs produce a powerful arousal or alerting action and exert their effects by similar chemical mechanisms in the central nervous system. While these drugs have been around for a long time, they have experienced a trade-off in terms of their popularity over the last thirty years. Amphetamine appears to have been more popular in the 1960's and 1970's, with cocaine more or less replacing amphetamine as the stimulant of choice in the 1980's.[3] However, both drugs continue to be abused in significant amounts by young people.

The most desired street form of amphetamine is methamphetamine, which has acquired the name crank.

Methamphetamine (which involves a simple modification of the amphetamine chemical structure) appears to have a greater central nervous system potency and provides a "bigger bang for the buck" than does amphetamine. On the street, methamphetamine has typically been available in liquid ampule form of injection, although it can be obtained in other forms as well.

There is also clear evidence that repeated use of amphetamine-like stimulants produces both physical and psychological dependence. That is to say, withdrawal symptoms occur several hours after the last dose of the drug and the drug becomes habit-forming to the abuser. Most frightening of all is the fact that, with large doses of amphetamine-like drugs, the abuser could experience what is called "amphetamine psychosis".[4] This condition is described as a schizophrenia-like state accompanied by auditory or visual hallucinations (false perceptions). Such an effect is frightening to the abuser and may lead him to believe he is "going crazy". Fortunately, this is a temporary condition and usually disappears when the drug effect wears off. Amphetamine-like drugs are potentially dangerous and should be avoided by all young people.

Cocaine, an extract of the South American coca plant, has increasingly become the stimulant of choice by drug abusers. This drug is typically "snorted" (sniffed through the nasal cavity) although on occasion it might be injected intravenously. The latter route of introduction to the body produces a rapid and powerful effect which is brief and may be accompanied by a "crash" sensation when the effect wears off.

Freebasing of cocaine (heating a mixture of cocaine with baking soda and water) markedly increases the potency of the drug with the end product referred to as crack or rock. This form of the drug is typically inhaled as a volatile substance and is the choice of abusers who are in need of a stronger kick in order to maintain the drug's effectiveness. There is no doubt that, as is the case with amphetamine-like products, cocaine also produces both physical and psychological dependence. Indeed, dependence develops rapidly with the crack or rock form of cocaine which may very well explain the popularity of this form of the drug.

Opiates: The poppy of the opium plant is the source of several naturally occurring opiate drugs, the most popular ones being morphine and codeine. Such drugs are referred to as narcotics[5] because of their effectiveness in reducing pain and dulling the senses.

Heroin is a synthetic opiate produced by a slight modification of the morphine molecule and is, by far, the most addicting and abused of the opiate drugs. Heroin (Horse, Big H) is considered by many to be the most popular illicit drug available and can be ingested, inhaled, smoked, snorted or injected. The preferred route of administration is intravenous injection (also called mainlining), which produces an almost immediate effect, often referred to as a "rush".

The general effects produced by heroin include: loss of pain sensation, drowsiness and euphoria (a psychological sense of well-being). The latter effect is, undoubtedly, a major reason for the drug's popularity. These effects are apparently brought about by the drug's action on chemical systems in the central nervous system. Heroin produces both physical and psychological dependence and is considered by some professionals to be the "model par excellence" of drug addiction.[6]

This reputation should be enough to convince anyone that it is an extremely dangerous drug and should be avoided by all young people. Parenthetically, because heroin is so addictive, the chance of overdosing on the drug is very real. In such a case, emergency medical treatment may require the use of other drugs which block the action of heroin (Narcan or Trexan).

Hallucinogens: Drugs falling under this category share in common the properties of producing distortions in the perception of reality and hallucinations. They are, in many respects, a "mixed bag" of substances in spite of the fact that they share common properties. Lysergic acid diethylamide (LSD) is the most potent of the hallucinogens and is the standard by which all others are measured.

Two other hallucinogens that will be briefly considered include phencyclidine (PCP) and mescaline. LSD (acid) was first isolated from the ergot fungus of infected cereal grains. Since that time, it has been synthesized in many different laboratories (both official and clandestine) and appears on the streets in this form. LSD is almost always administered orally and because it is so powerful, only a tiny amount is needed to produce its mind-altering effects. In spite of the pronounced psychological effects of LSD, the drug does not appear to produce any serious dependence, either physical or psychological.[7] Thus, in one sense, it may be a relatively safe drug compared to many others that are abused.

However, there are serious effects associated with the drug experience that provide ample reason to avoid its use. Panic reactions (extreme anxiety attacks) frequently occur and some abusers report the experience of synesthesia, a mixing of the senses.[8] With such an experience, a person may "see" sounds or "hear" colors with this only adding to the disorientation produced by the drug.

More critical than this is the frightening experience of flashbacks. Weeks or months after a person has taken LSD, he may experience a recurrence of symptoms. While the exact reason for such experiences is not clear, this should by itself be enough to encourage young people to stay away from the drug.

Other hallucinogens include PCP (angel dust) and mescaline (buttons). PCP is a very unpredictable drug which was originally used as an animal anesthetic. As a drug of abuse, PCP is commonly smoked, although it can be introduced into the body by other methods as well. The drug produces a state of delirium which in many respects resembles schizophrenia. The disorganized thinking, suspiciousness and lack of cooperation of the PCP abuser makes him a physical threat to himself as well as those surrounding him. In contrast to other hallucinogens, there is also some evidence that PCP produces some form of dependence as well.[9]

These facts, coupled with PCP abuse being the most common cause of drug-induced visits to hospital emergency rooms, indicate that the drug is extremely dangerous. Indeed, it may be the most dangerous drug of abuse available on the street and young people should avoid it at all cost.

Mescaline (derived from the crown of the peyote cactus) is a drug that produces effects similar to, but much less pronounced than those of LSD. With high doses in particular a full set of auditory and tactile (touch) hallucinations occur, as is quite typical with LSD. Also, these hallucinations are frequently accompanied by synesthetic experiences. However, with low doses, the effects are rather benign and involve mainly a sense of euphoria.

Mescaline is consumed orally as part of the prepared cactus crown (mescal buttons) and does not appear to be as dangerous a drug as the two preceding hallucinogens. However, it is not used without hazards and should be avoided by young people as a matter of precaution and common sense.

Marijuana: While there is some controversy as to whether marijuana should be defined as a hallucinogen, it probably has more in common with this type of drug than most. Marijuana is a preparation of leafy material from the plant Cannabis Sativa and is typically smoked. Its primary active ingredient is tetrahydrocannabinol (THC) which is concentrated mainly in the resin of the flowering tops of the plants. The average potency of marijuana found in Cannabis plants is approximately 2-5% THC. Hashish is a purer form of marijuana and may contain from 7-14% THC and boiling the plants in alcohol and filtering out the solids (hash oil) may increase the level of THC to as much as 50%.[10]

The psychological effects of marijuana appear to involve several phases, but, in general, are described as a state of daydreaming.[11] Such effects include feelings of hilarity followed by a mood of carefree relaxation, drowsiness and mild euphoria. While most of these effects are reported to be emotionally pleasing to young abusers, there is some evidence that such enjoyment has to be learned. Marijuana appears to produce both psychological and physical dependence, although evidence for the latter is less than conclusive at the present time.

One of the most serious effects of marijuana abuse is the phenomenon called "amotivational syndrome".[12] Characteristics of this syndrome include apathy, lack of motivation and general loss of interest in achievement. One can see quite clearly how such an effect can have a marked impact on the scholastic activity of teenagers or on their job performance. The physiological effects of marijuana, particularly on the cardiovascular system, have been likened to those of cigarette smoking and hardly constitute an endorsement of the drug.[13]

On balance, smoking marijuana is not the harmless experience it is made out to be. Whatever pleasure one might derive from the drug is obtained at an unacceptable cost—both psychologically and physically.

Anabolic steroids: The male sex hormone testosterone has several types of effects on the developing male. Several of these effects have to do with specific development of the sex organs, deepening of the voice and appearance of facial hair. However, other effects of the male sex hormone promote the metabolism and building of muscle tissue. It is this latter type of effect that is captured by anabolic steroids. Such steroids are modified chemical structures of testosterone that are designed specifically to build muscle mass without producing many of the other effects normally associated with testosterone. Such drugs are typically taken by young body builders and other athletes in order to enhance their performance. The critical question is, "Do they, in fact, enhance athletic ability?"

While anabolic steroids undoubtedly increase strength, there is some serious question about their ability to significantly enhance activity. The young male athlete already has a high level of testosterone circulating in his body and adding a little more to this is probably not going to have a significant effect. However, since the outcome of many athletic events is decided by fractions of a second, such added strength could determine the difference between winning and losing. It is this little edge that many athletes, particularly sprinters, are seeking.

Whatever slight advantage there might be to the athlete, it is achieved at a tremendous cost, both psychologically and physically. Such hormones can produce an increase in aggressive acts and feelings of violence, as well as damaging the liver, increasing blood pressure and potentially causing heart disease.[14] It is quite obvious that these drugs are extremely dangerous and should be avoided by all young people, including the most ardent athlete.

Designer drugs: The illicit drug scene is constantly undergoing change as a result of federal laws designed to regulate the illegal drug markets. In order to stay one step ahead of the government, many illegal laboratories have synthesized new products or modified existing illicit drugs. Collectively, such drugs are known as designer drugs.

In many respects, these drugs are more dangerous than existing illicit drugs since much less may be known about their psychological and physiological effects. For example, the designer drug commonly known as ecstasy (a hallucinogenic amphetamine) produces very powerful psychological effects; however, questions about its origin, strength and purity make it extremely dangerous. Perhaps the greatest recorded tragedy associated with designer drugs is that related to a heroin substitute (MPTP) produced by an underground chemist in California.[15]

A number of young drug abusers who took the drug developed brain damage and symptoms of Parkinson's disease (tremors and lack of motor control). These young people are marked for life and although the symptoms can be partially controlled with medication, they must contend with this irreversible condition. Because of the uncertainty factor associated with designer drugs, they are extremely dangerous and should be avoided at all cost.

Solvent inhalants: The inhaling of solvents (a gas or liquid substance containing intoxicating components) is a serious problem, especially among males in their teens.[16] These chemicals (e.g. airplane glue, gasoline, paint thinners, aerosols) are not regulated like most drugs of abuse and are readily available to young people. In fact, they are as close and accessible as your local garage or hardware store.

As is true with designer drugs, the potential for serious consequences is great. With low doses of solvents there may be some mild stimulation followed by a loss of control, lack of coordination and disorientation accompanied by dizziness. With higher doses, violent behavior may occur with the user possibly losing consciousness. If continued for a long period of time, solvent abuse may cause brain damage or result in death. Parents should be particularly cautious about making sure their children are not inadvertently exposed to such chemicals since such exposure could provide the opportunity for their abuse.

Concluding Comments

While any drug can be abused (legal or illegal), illicit drugs present a particular challenge and problem to those concerned about drug abuse among young people. Illicit drugs are the ones that "float" around our high schools and that are readily available on the streets of our towns and cities. Christian workers and parents are unlikely to know much about them or have any contact with the solicitation or distribution of such drugs. As a result, they are likely to feel a sense of frustration in knowing how to deal with such problems. However, this sense of frustration should not give way to despair. We need to be in touch with what is going on at school and in the streets of our neighborhoods.

One important thing adults can do is to learn more about the nature and effects of illicit drugs. This is where the present chapter may minister to you, for it is specifically designed to inform Christian workers and parents about the potential dangers associated with the most commonly abused illicit drugs. If it is successful in doing this, the present chapter may turn out to be the most important one in this book. Regardless of how you rank the importance of this chapter, it still provides valuable ammunition in the endless war against drugs. It is not only vital to have such information available, it is equally important that it be utilized in discussing problems of drug abuse with young people.

Parents, don't assume anything when it comes to your children and drug abuse. Use a frontal attack in dealing with such problems and don't wait for signs of a drug problem to develop. If you have taken advantage of such information on illicit drugs, your children or other young people are more likely to respect you and listen to what you have to say. Uninformed Christian workers and parents are not going to get very far in discussing problems of drug abuse with young people. The reason for this is relatively simple—young people are, in general, fairly sophisticated when it comes to drugs and expect the same from those who attempt to influence their decisions.

Hopefully, this chapter provides an equally clear message we should pass on to young people who are tempted to abuse illicit drugs or who may be in the early (experimental) stage of abuse. The message is simply this—there is absolutely no safe illicit drug available, no matter what you have been told by well-meaning or well-informed peers or adults. While the risk varies with the type of illicit drug, you pay a price with the abuse of all of them. In some instances, as it may very well be with PCP, this price could be your life.

In other cases, the price may seem so small that it is worth the risk. This is the attitude many teenagers have about marijuana. However, the momentary pleasant feelings experienced under the influence of marijuana must be weighed against the mental apathy and potential physiological harm associated with the drug. The problem with marijuana, as it is with many psychoactive drugs, is that the present drug-induced euphoria may cloud the broader picture thus blinding the teenager to the true cost of the experience. Teenagers need to be reminded of the broader picture from time to time in order to keep things in perspective.

If nothing else, it is hoped that after finishing this chapter, adults are more sensitive to the dangers associated with the abuse of illegal drugs by young people. Certainly, such drugs have no place in the life of the young Christian.

Key questions answered by this chapter include:

1. What is an illicit drug?
2. What patterns of abuse are associated with illicit drugs?
3. What is "crack" cocaine and why is it so dangerous?
4. Why is heroin such a popular illicit drug?
5. What are some of the immediate and long-term effects of LSD?
6. Is marijuana really a harmful drug?
7. What are the primary dangers associated with anabolic steroids?
8. What is a designer drug?
9. What is the danger of inhaling solvents?
10. How can we help to stem the influence of illicit drugs?

Notes

Chapter Thirteen

Unrecognized Drugs

Have you ever heard someone say, "I may drink and smoke but I most certainly do not use drugs." This is a common response people give when questioned about such behavior and points out the major problem with defining a drug. As a general rule, society does not define chemical substances as drugs on the basis of their pharmacological action or their potential danger. Rather, such substances tend to be defined in terms of their legal status or general availability. If they are illegal and not readily available, you can get most people to agree that the substance must be a drug. However, if it is legal and readily available to the general public, most people would hesitate to call the substance a drug. Such is the case with alcohol and nicotine (the active substance found in tobacco products). Since it is legal to purchase and use them (provided one meets the minimum age requirement) and they can be found in nearly every store, they are not recognized as drugs.

The problem is further augmented by the fact that both alcohol and nicotine (mainly cigarettes) are also seen by many as social facilitators and adjuncts to "the good life". A cocktail before dinner, a glass of wine with dinner and a cigarette after dinner are seen by many as the hallmark of good taste and a symbol of one's social sophistication. Granted, it is becoming increasingly difficult for the smoker to light up in public places; however, alcohol consumption is still a popular pastime in most restaurants (the not-so-classy as well as the classy) and the smoker will eventually have a cigarette. Society tends to condone such behavior largely because it cannot adequately control it. It is a classic example of the old adage, "If you can't beat them, join them." Historically, attempts to make the manufacturing, distribution and use of alcohol illegal have failed miserably.[1]

In the same manner, while the federal government's anti-smoking program for the past 25-30 years has met with some success,[2] a significant segment of the population in this country still smokes. Whatever the public attitudes about alcohol and nicotine, it is time to "call a spade a spade". The purpose of this chapter is to demonstrate that both alcohol and nicotine have powerful pharmacological effects and should be treated as drugs by young people and adults.

Alcohol

The alcohol consumed in beverages is ethyl alcohol (Ethanol) with its strength determined by the processes of fermentation and distillation. Fermentation is the starting point for all alcoholic beverages and is produced by the action of certain yeasts on sugar in the presence of water. Most fruits (e.g., grapes) and cereal grains (e.g., barley) contain sugar or starch that can be converted to sugar and thus provide ample sources for the production of alcohol. As a process, fermentation is able to produce an alcohol content of 10-15%. This is quite adequate for many alcoholic beverages, including beer (4-5%) and most wines (7-10%).

In order to obtain alcohol concentrations higher than those resulting from fermentation, distillation is required. In this process, the solution containing alcohol is heated and the vapors of this process are collected and condensed into liquid form. Distillation can increase the alcoholic content of a beverage up to 40-50% or even higher in some instances. The alcoholic content of distilled beverages is defined by its proof—twice the actual alcoholic content by volume. For example, 90 proof would be 45% alcohol. Distilled beverages include the so-called "hard liquors" such as brandy, whisky, gin and vodka.

From the above discussion, it should be quite obvious that the effects of alcoholic beverages depend upon the amount of alcohol in a drink. It is also the case that such effects depend upon how frequently one drinks. One valuable measure of the combined effects of the amount and frequency of alcohol consumption is the blood alcohol level (BAL). The BAL is a good indicator of the amount of alcohol in the body and a sensitive index of the degree of impairment produced by alcohol. For example, a BAL of 0.10 defines legal intoxication in most states,[3] and anyone driving a motor vehicle under such conditions has seriously impaired reaction time and perceptual-motor skills. Unfortunately, the majority of people caught driving under the influence of alcohol (DUI) are young people (ages 16-22),[4] a fact about which we should be greatly concerned.

Since the body metabolizes alcohol at a constant rate, drinking large amounts of alcoholic beverages in a relatively short period of time can increase the BAL well above the level of legal intoxication. In such instances, one can expect a further impairment in motor functions, a marked depression of sensory capacity and possibly even a stuporous condition (decreased awareness of what is going on). An equally important fact is that how one feels is not a good measure of the actual impact alcohol is having on a person. Feelings can be very deceptive and mislead people into believing that they are in control when, in fact, they are not. Young people are particularly vulnerable to such deception.

Alcohol is a central nervous system depressant and as such produces a general sedation action. While the exact mechanism underlying the drug's action is not clear, it probably produces its effects by acting on the same central systems involved in the action of prescription anti-anxiety drugs (see Chapter 10). This, again, is the main reason it is so dangerous to drink alcoholic beverages while taking anti-anxiety or similar medication. Their combined effects can be life-threatening, particularly in the case of a depression of respiration.

One other unfortunate factor associated with the depressant action of alcohol is the manner in which it affects social inhibitions. Alcohol tends to decrease social inhibitions, making promiscuous thoughts and actions more likely. While all of us need to recognize the potential danger associated with such changes, our young people in particular need to be cautioned about such effects. They are facing enough problems without creating a situation that only intensifies their struggle.

In addition to the powerful effects of chronic alcoholism, the drug's short-term effects are equally dangerous. Alcohol can induce blackouts—periods of time during alcohol use when the individual does not lose consciousness but cannot recall events at a later date when sober.[5] Many authorities consider such a selective memory loss with blackouts to be a serious danger sign and indicative of excessive alcohol use. Alcohol also increases aggression and the likelihood of violent actions. It has been estimated that, in about half of the homicide cases, the killer, the victim or both have measurable BALs.[6]

Furthermore, it is estimated that alcohol is involved in about one-third of all suicides. It appears that alcoholism is second only to depression as a cause in suicide attempts by young people. This should not be surprising since many young people drink because they are depressed or vice versa.

Finally, alcohol may produce birth defects in an unborn child of an expectant mother. The most common type of such a defect is called "fetal alcohol syndrome" (FAS).[7] Alcohol in the bloodstream of a mother who drinks passes freely across the placenta, enters the unborn baby's bloodstream and causes serious damage to the developing fetus, particularly the brain. This syndrome results in growth retardation, abnormal facial features, brain abnormalities and below average intellectual functioning. Such a condition is particularly tragic in the case of young mothers who may face an uncertain future with the care of such a child.

While there is no one specific cause of alcoholism, attempts to explain why people drink include many of the same influences associated with drug abuse in general (see Chapter 2). However, two factors in particular appear to be of interest in the case of alcoholism—psycho-social influences and genetic predispositions. Regarding the former, young people may drink because they possess certain personality traits which make them more susceptible to alcoholism.[8] While personality traits may contribute to a drinking problem, one should not emphasize such factors to the exclusion of other psycho-social influences. Some young people may drink simply because they observe their parents doing so in the home or because they are pressured to do so by their peers. In such cases, it is easy for the novice drinker to lose his sense of self-control and become increasingly vulnerable to alcoholism.

There is also increasing evidence that alcoholism may, in part, be inherited. Alcoholism tends to run in families and people who are closely related genetically (e.g., identical twins) are more likely to share drinking problems than individuals who are not genetically related. Undoubtedly, multiple factors contribute to alcoholism; however, because a strong dependency (both physical and psychological) develops with alcohol, the underlying cause of alcoholism is not a moot point. With all things being equal, a young person with a possible genetic predisposition to alcoholism runs an increased risk of developing a drinking problem. If there is a drinking problem in the immediate family or with a close relative, that young person would do well to take special precaution to avoid the use of alcohol.

Nicotine

While tobacco smoking in some form has a long recorded history (at least 400-500 years),[9] cigarette smoking is the most recent way to use tobacco and will be the main focus of our discussion. Furthermore, cigarette smoking deserves the greatest attention, since it is the most toxic way to use tobacco. One of the major tobaccos used in the manufacturing of cigarettes is the Burley plant, which has a nicotine content ranging from 0.3-7%.[10] After harvesting, the tobacco leaves of the Burley plant are cured and aged prior to technology taking over the process of manufacturing the final product—rolled cigarettes.

Nicotine (the psycho-active substance in cigarettes) is potentially a deadly drug and has a biphasic (two phases) action on areas of the central and peripheral nervous systems. Initially, the drug has a stimulating or arousal effect on these sites; however, after this initial excitement, the drug tends to produce a calming or tranquilizing effect. This dual action of the drug appears to be due to an initial activation of certain receptors in the nervous system, followed by a blocking of these same receptors.

In the stimulating or arousal phase, nicotine increases both the heart rate and blood pressure. Because of the carbon monoxide contained in cigarettes, the heart also becomes deprived of oxygen in the process of arousal. Another related negative effect of nicotine is its tendency to increase blood clotting, an effect which only further impedes the flow of blood. As a result of these combined actions, nicotine markedly increases the risk of a heart attack and cardiovascular disease. Nicotine also activates a hormone from the adrenal gland that only further increases this arousal action.

The calming action following this period of arousal is characterized by a reduction in activity (both physiologically and behaviorally) and may be an important part of the reinforcing effect of the drug. Such short spells of tranquility may be characterized by a sense of relief from stress or even a feeling of euphoria. As is the case with alcohol, nicotine is a highly addictive drug (both physically and psychologically) and attempts to "cure" smoking have met with mixed results. Young people who say they can quit any time they want, usually find themselves "hooked" for life. While numerous techniques have been used in the treatment of smoking (e.g., nicotine patch and pills, behavior reinforcement, etc.), those who are motivated to quit on their own appear to do better than those who have been in a specific treatment program.[11]

Although the primary focus of this section is on nicotine, it is important to recognize that cigarette tobacco also contains other potentially dangerous substances. These include tar (complex mixture of chemicals), carbon monoxide (gas which deprives the blood of oxygen) and potent carcinogens (cancer-producing agents). Particularly when tobacco is burned, these substances are a major cause of lung cancer, coronary heart disease and numerous health-related complications. Combined with nicotine, these substances not only produce further negative consequences on the smoker but have an even more devastating effect on the unborn babies of smokers. Smoking during pregnancy may produce a reduction in birth weight, cause spontaneous abortion and have long-lasting effects on the intellectual and physical development of the child. The reduced availability of oxygen to the developing fetus is responsible for most of these tragic effects. Young expecting mothers, in particular, need to be warned of such dangers.

Not only is smoking a health hazard to the smoker but cigarette smoke is increasingly being recognized as a health hazard to non-smokers as well. Non-smokers who passively inhale smoke from the environment are exposed to the same health risks as smokers. The risk to non-smokers appears to be particularly high in the case of "sidestream smoke".[12] In such a case, smoke rising from the ashes of a burning cigarette is probably higher in harmful substances than the primary smoke inhaled by the smoker.

Because of the protest of many non-smokers, this issue of "passive smoking" has led to a serious conflict between the rights of an individual to smoke and general concerns for public health. Should the rights of an individual to jeopardize his own health also include the right to jeopardize the health of those who choose to be around them? Society's general response to this question has been, "No!" Increasingly, we have seen more restrictions placed on smoking in workplaces and public facilities, with this trend likely to continue in the near future.

While most people recognize that smoking is a health hazard, attempts by health-conscious agencies (e.g., American Cancer Society, American Medical Association, etc.) to curb such behavior frequently go unheeded. This is due, largely, to the fact that the economics of the tobacco industry make smoking a political issue as well as a health issue.[13] Making and selling tobacco in this country is a highly profitable business, and many people depend upon the tobacco industry for their livelihood, either directly or indirectly. Taking tobacco off the market would not only deprive the tobacco farmer of making a living from the tobacco crop, but also have a negative economic impact on those who manufacture the product and sell it through thousands of retail outlets. As we have seen in recent Congressional hearings, the tobacco industry is ably represented in our Nation's Capitol and is not about to let that happen. As a general rule, politicians and the tobacco industry are much more concerned about their own welfare than they are about the welfare of our children.

Although cigarette smoking is generally recognized as a serious health hazard, it is also a preventable cause of death. It has been estimated that every cigarette steals seven minutes of a smoker's life and that 20% of all U.S. deaths in 1990 were attributed to cigarette smoking. In spite of the shocking nature of these findings, there are still approximately 46 million smokers in this country.[14] It is not surprising that one author claims, "Tobacco is America's true 'killer weed' and is a bigger public health threat than all other drug substances combined."[15]

While some may question such a claim, it is true, nevertheless, that smoking adversely affects the lives of too many people. While some smokers claim that there are benefits associated with cigarette smoking (e.g., stress release, appetite suppression, etc.), these benefits are achieved at an unacceptably high cost. Furthermore, it is now recognized that nicotine has no medically-accepted therapeutic use. In fact, it primarily functions as a poison with a dose as low as 60 milligrams being fatal in most instances.[16]

Fortunately, the inhaled smoke of cigarettes does not contain such levels of the drug. Also, any attempt to lower the health risk by smoking low tar/nicotine cigarettes tends to be self-defeating. The smoker usually aims at a certain nicotine level and simply smokes more to compensate for the reduction. No matter how you look at it, the bottom line is that cigarette smoking does not do anybody (young or old) any good, under any conditions.

In addition to cigarette smoking, one major problem among young males, in particular, is the increased use of so-called smokeless (chewing) tobacco. The increase is partially due to an effective and persistent advertising campaign, showing famous athletes using such products. This is particularly true with baseball players (and their managers) depicted on television as the tough guys of summer sports. It is very easy for young males to identify with the success of such individuals and begin to pattern their behavior after them.

Unfortunately, however, the link between chewing tobacco and health hazards is seriously understated or ignored entirely. Such tobacco is usually sold in a can (e.g., Copenhagen, Skoal) and a small pinch of it is usually placed beside the gums, often behind the lower lip. With all forms of such tobacco, nicotine is readily absorbed through the mucous membrane of the mouth. Thus, all of the harmful effects of nicotine associated with smoking pertain here as well. Chewing tobacco also contains potent carcinogens and many users experience tissue changes in the mouth (a thickening and hardening of tissue) that may lead to precancerous sores.[17] It is quite obvious that, along with cigarette smoking, the use of chewing tobacco represents a significant health hazard to our young people.

Concluding comments

If the message of this chapter hits home, I trust that it is received in the right spirit and will provide new insight into the potential dangers of alcohol and cigarettes (nicotine) to our young people in particular. I suspect that this chapter will not change many minds, and I am willing to accept that fact. If, however, it causes you to reassess your own ideas about these drugs and their potentially harmful effects, this is enough.

Some would remind us that while alcohol is frequently abused, it also may have some medical benefits in moderate doses. We have all heard that a glass of wine each day may have some beneficial effects in preventing clogged arteries and heart attacks.

While I might be the first to recognize the potential medical benefits of moderate amounts of alcohol, the problem becomes that of defining what one means by moderation. In attempting to define the term, let us ask three social drinkers what they mean by moderation. Do we need to proceed any further? It is quite obvious that we are likely to get three different answers since each has an idea of what moderation means. Reactions to such a question are based upon the personal experience of each of our social drinkers; thus, it is virtually impossible to come up with a working, general definition of moderation acceptable to all.

What, then, does it mean to say that it is acceptable to drink in moderation? This is a question not only for our secular friends, but one for Christians as well. It is becoming increasing acceptable in Christian circles (including some evangelical circles) to share a glass of wine during social events. Many Christians have the attitude that the negative evidence associated with alcohol use is reserved for the secular world and that the label of "teetotaler" is passé and out of step with progressive Christianity. While this chapter is not designed to instruct Christians as to whether they should or should not drink socially, I trust that it will at least provide the rationale for some to say, "No, thank you" and not feel threatened in doing so.

My feelings regarding cigarette smoking (and other forms of tobacco use) are, however, less understanding. Knowing what we do about the health hazards of nicotine and other substances in tobacco, there is absolutely no basis on which one can justify smoking. Unlike alcohol, there are no known beneficial effects associated with smoking,[18] regardless of whether or not it is low or moderate in nature. We need to drive this point home to our young people.

The general tendency has been to emphasize the war on drugs and in the process, to exclude alcohol and nicotine. This double standard of talking about drugs while being quiet about alcohol and nicotine, gives mixed messages to our young people in particular. While the use of both alcohol and nicotine is interwoven into the fabric of the American society, we must recognize the need to address these issues if we ever hope to get a handle on problems of drug abuse.

Alcohol and nicotine have been around for a long time. However, I am convinced of one important fact—if they were newly discovered drugs about to be marketed today, they would both be defined as controlled substances and would not be made available to the general public. If nothing else, think on that fact. Hopefully, that fact will also influence any personal decisions we make about alcohol and nicotine and what we teach our children about these drugs.

Key questions answered by this chapter include:

1. Why aren't alcohol and nicotine (tobacco) recognized as drugs?
2. What does the blood-alcohol level measure?
3. Does alcohol increase aggression and attempts at suicide?
4. Can the risk of alcoholism be increased by genetic influences?
5. What is the nature of nicotine's dual action on the body?
6. Can cigarette smoking be harmful to non-smokers?
7. Does nicotine have any beneficial or therapeutic use?
8. Is chewing tobacco dangerous?
9. What is the problem with drinking alcohol in moderation?

Notes

Appendix A

Principles Of Drug Action

This section is designed to provide the reader with some supplemental information on the nature of drugs and their action. If more detail is desired, a number of good secular sources are available. The information provided here is intended to be of a more general nature and simply a starting point for the interested reader.

Generic vs. Brand Name Drugs

The generic name of a drug is the official name of the drug and can be used by anyone, since it is not protected by trademark laws. In contrast, the brand (or trade) name of a drug specifies a particular manufacturer of a generic product.

Under the federal trademark protection laws, a manufacturer of a drug is given 17 years to manufacture and sell that drug without competition. When this protection period runs out, the drug becomes "free game" and can be produced by any manufacturer that has the capacity to do so. Another pharmaceutical company may choose to manufacture and sell the drug under its own brand name or to market the drug under the generic name.

Competition among pharmaceutical firms characteristically decreases the cost of the product and can create a significant savings to the public. Generic drugs are required by federal law to be equivalent in every respect to the brand drug manufactured and sold by the original company.

How Do Drugs Get into the Body?

In order for any drug to have an effect on the brain or other parts of the body it must, first of all, get into the body. While drug abusers have some ingenious ways of introducing illegal drugs, there are two traditional ways of taking drugs—orally and by injection. Taking drugs orally (by mouth) is undoubtedly the oldest and easiest way to administer drugs. However, it is not necessarily the most effective route of administration. Not only does the drug have to be absorbed from the digestive tract (stomach or intestines), but it is also affected by the presence of food substances in the digestive system.

In contrast to oral administration, taking drugs by injection is more varied in its approach. In human patients, there are three primary means of injection—intravenous, subcutaneous and intramuscular. With intravenous injection, the drug is introduced directly into the blood stream and thus does not have to be absorbed from some tissue area. As a result, the onset of the drug's action is faster than by any other means of injection.

Subcutaneous injection involves administering the drug directly under the skin. This means of introducing a drug is sometimes called "skin popping" by the drug abuser and is not, as a rule, used in common medical practice, except for sensitivity tests. Drugs injected in this manner can be irritating to the skin tissue and are absorbed slowly.

The final major injection route is that of intramuscular injection. Injections of this type are frequently given in the deltoid muscle of the arm or other muscles which have a good blood supply. The drug is absorbed rapidly and has an onset of effect that is almost as rapid as that of intravenous injections. Most of the "shots" given to patients by physicians are intramuscular injections because this route of getting drugs into the body is both safe and effective.

Other less popular and less regulated techniques of administrating drugs are also worthy of mention. The application of some drugs by means of a skin patch may be an effective way to provide a slow, steady supply of the drug over a period of time. Nicotine patches may be of help to people who are trying to quit smoking by preventing relapses. Other drugs are absorbed directly from the mucous membrane of the mouth region, which has a rich blood supply. This is the case with so-called smokeless tobaccos (chewing tobacco). Rectal or vaginal suppositories are another way of getting drugs into the body. Tissue in these body regions is richly supplied by blood and drugs are readily absorbed by this means. Suppositories are particularly popular with drug abusers that may have collapsed veins as a result of repeated intravenous injection. Finally, snorting or sniffing certain drugs is popular among cocaine users because of the ease and effectiveness of such a route. However, the nasal membranes are very sensitive and repeated use of this type can seriously irritate or damage nasal passages.

What Happens to Drugs in the Body?

Once drugs get into the body by some means of administration, they undergo a dynamic process of change. This process involves several stages from the time of entrance to the time of exit.

Initially, drugs must be absorbed from some tissue site in order to reach the blood stream. As was indicated in the previous section, drugs injected intravenously do not need to be absorbed because they are already in the blood stream. The rate of absorption from other areas of administration depends upon blood supply to the area as well as other factors. Generally, intramuscular injections are absorbed more rapidly than either subcutaneous injection or oral administration.

Once the drug enters the blood stream, it is distributed throughout the body. Many drugs may bind to substances in the blood plasma and are carried "piggy back" to their final destination. While most drugs have some effect on all areas of the body, the primary site of their action may be located in the brain or spinal cord (central nervous system) or some area outside these sites (peripheral nervous system).

Although drugs can freely influence activity in the peripheral nervous system, their influence on activity in the central nervous system is much more selective. This is due to a physiological mechanism called the blood brain barrier. While this is not a literal barrier, it does describe a process by which drugs have selective access to brain areas. Psychoactive drugs, which are those most typically abused, are able to pass this barrier and, thus, have significant effects on the brain.

Psychoactive drugs do not usually influence the whole brain, but, rather, produce their effects by acting on a specific location in the central nervous system. This location is called the "target site" of the drug. Such target sites of drugs are associated with specific areas of the nervous system called the synapse. The word "synapse" literally means gap and is descriptive of the fact that cells in the central nervous system (called neurons) do not communicate with each other by direct physical contact. Rather, they communicate with each other by releasing chemicals called transmitters. These transmitters are released at the synapse, and most psychoactive drugs produce their effects by altering, in some manner, their action.

The effect of different psychoactive drugs on transmitters can become a complex picture, since there are numerous types of transmitters and drugs can alter various stages of transmitter activity. In some cases, drugs may also produce effects similar to those of the transmitter (called agonistic effects), while, in other instances, they may produce effects that actually block the action of the transmitter (called antagonistic effects). Such a blocking action should not be viewed as a negative event, since drugs that are used to treat the very serious symptoms of schizophrenia have their beneficial results by blocking the action of one such transmitter.

After drugs have had their effects on transmitters, they are metabolized (broken down) and excreted from the body in the final stage of their dynamic journey. Kidney excretion of drugs is the primary way in which they are removed from the body, although small amounts of the drug may also be excreted through feces and respiration. Kidney functions, and thus the ability to excrete drugs, vary considerably with age and appear to decline after middle age. Because of this decline in renal function with age, elderly patients represent a special challenge with drug treatment.

Drug Tolerance

As drugs move through the body and undergo change so also does the body undergo change. One of the most vivid examples of this change has to do with the concept of tolerance. In general, tolerance can be defined as a reduced response of the body to a drug with its repeated use. Such a reduced response to the drug is due to two specific changes in the body. One of these is the result of the drug's target site becoming less sensitive to the drug's action with its repeated stimulation. This effect is called "cellular tolerance", referring to the fact that it is associated with changes taking place in the cells of the nervous system.

Another important change the body undergoes with repeated drug use is related to liver action. With repeated use, the liver produces more enzymes which break the drug down more quickly, thus reducing the effectiveness of the drug. This effect is called "dispositional tolerance" since it relates to the overall disposition (fate) of the drug.

Building up tolerance to one drug can actually carry over to another drug having similar properties. This is called "cross tolerance" and becomes particularly critical in the treatment of some conditions with medication. Someone who is a heavy alcohol drinker may actually build up a tolerance to other drugs having similar sedative or relaxing effects. Needless to say, this could make the legitimate medication less effective and create serious problems in the management of such medication.

Drug Addiction

As currently viewed, addiction includes some combination of tolerance, physical dependence and psychological dependence. Tolerance has already been discussed in the preceding section. Physical dependence is defined in terms of a collection of symptoms caused by the drug's removal and are known as withdrawal symptoms. While the critical nature of the symptoms may vary with the drug, they typically include diarrhea, sweating, headaches, rapid heart rate as well as other serious effects.

Apparently the individual's body has compensated for the presence of the drug with repeated use and such changes produce an imbalance when the drug is removed.

While the medical profession has tended to focus on physical dependency, it has become increasingly clear that addiction includes important psychological factors as well. Collectively, such factors are referred to as "psychological dependence". This aspect of addiction would include a strong craving for a drug as well as other aspects of "drug-seeking" behavior. Drugs that produce the most powerful reinforcing effects have the greatest potential for producing psychological dependence. Recent views on addiction suggest that the driving force behind addictive behavior may depend more on psychological factors than on physical factors.

Drug Safety

The general safety of drugs used for clinical purposes is determined by what is called the therapeutic index. In order to calculate this index, one must first identify two other important measures of a drug's effect. The median effective dose (that dose which produces the desired effect in the subjects tested) must be determined along with the median lethal dose (that dose which produces death in the subjects studied). Animals are obviously used to determine the latter measure, and the results are extrapolated to the human level.

The therapeutic index (also called the margin of safety) is then calculated by dividing the median lethal dose by the median effective dose. The larger the number resulting from such a calculation, the greater the margin of safety one has in using a particular drug. Suppose, for example, that drug A has a median effective dose of 5 milligrams and a median lethal dose of 20 milligrams. In contrast, let us say drug B has a median effective dose of 4 milligrams and a median lethal dose of 8 milligrams. Which of these drugs has the greatest margin of safety in its use? In the case of drug A, 20/5=4; whereas, with drug B, 8/4=2. It is quite apparent that drug A has approximately twice the margin of safety in its use. Such a determination is critical for clinical practices and serves as a basis for physicians choosing one drug over another in the treatment of an illness.

Note

Most of the information in this section is obtained from several primary secular sources, which are highly recommended by the author. These sources are: David Grilly. *Drugs and Human Behavior* (Boston: Allyn and Bacon, 1989), Chapter 3; Oakey Ray and Charles Ksir. *Drugs, Society, & Human Behavior,* 5th Ed. (St. Louis: Times Mirror/Mosby, 1990), Chapter 6; and James Kalat. *Biological Psychology,* 5th Ed. (Pacific Grove, CA: Brooks/Cole Pub., 1995), Chapter 3.

Appendix B

Drug Classification

I am sure we have all heard the expression, "It's a jungle out there." Well, nowhere is that statement more true than when it comes to the world of drug information. The sheer volume of drug information, to say nothing of the complexity, is enough to totally overwhelm even the most interested person. Nobody really knows how many legitimate drugs there are on the market today (in addition to illicit ones), but it would certainly number several thousand. This is quite phenomenal when you consider the fact that such a spiraling availability of drugs has occurred within the relatively short period of 40 years. While modern clinical pharmacology really began in the 1950's, the volume of available drugs is presently so great that it becomes essential to classify or categorize them in a manner that makes some sense out of their use and effects.

I wish I could say that drug classification is easy and that everyone agrees as to how it should be done. Unfortunately, nothing is further from the truth. The classifying of drugs is different and, in many cases, no sharp distinction can be made between one class and another. Whatever specific type of drug classification one uses, it is important to keep in mind that it is arbitrary and serves only the purpose and needs of the classifier. One person's classification may be another person's folly.

All attempts to classify drugs are not, necessarily, meant to serve a broad audience. For example, an attorney might be quite content to simply classify all drugs as either legal or illegal. For purposes of interpreting the law, this is the only distinction that has a bearing on legal proceedings. In the same manner, the street user of drugs might only be interested in whether a particular drug produces an up-experience or a down-experience, not in other details about its effects. After all, street users tend to select drugs on the basis of their psychological and emotional impact and worry very little about the legal or illegal status of such substances.

While all types of drug classification are arbitrary, most have more substance than the examples mentioned above. This will become quite clear as we now turn to two classification approaches having the greatest influence on drug treatment and policies.

Controlled Substance Schedule

The Federal Government's comprehensive classification of drugs has its origin in the Controlled Substance Act of 1970. The law specifically states that drugs controlled by this act are under federal jurisdiction, making federal enforcement and prosecution possible whenever such drugs are involved in illegal activity. This act was an obvious attempt to put some muscle in the federal drug enforcement policies of the 1970's and was designed to separate enforcement from decisions made by the scientific and medical communities about which drugs should be controlled.

The act established five schedules of drugs based upon two specific criteria: a) the potential medical use of the drug; and b) the degree of potential for abuse and dependence associated with the drug. A drug assigned to Schedule I was assumed to have no known or accepted medical use and to have the highest probable risk for abuse and dependence. Drugs such as heroin and LSD are appropriately assigned to this schedule, although there is some question as to whether marijuana belongs here.

Drugs assigned to Schedules II through IV have various medical uses and a successively decreasing risk for abuse and dependence. Examples of drugs falling in this schedule range include: Amphetamine (II), Testosterone (III), and Valium (IV). While the present assignment of the two popular anti-anxiety drugs Librium and Valium to Schedule IV implies they have a low risk of potential for abuse and dependence, there is a growing concern about such an assumption.

Drugs assigned to Schedule V include those containing small amounts of narcotics. While some of these medicines (e.g., cough medicine) contain low doses of codeine, they are, as a group, considered to have little risk for abuse and dependence.

One of the most striking features of the federal scheduling of drugs is the penalties associated with violation of the Controlled Substance Act. First time offenders involved in the illegal use of Schedule I and II drugs can in theory receive up to 15 years in prison and be fined $25,000. Penalties are doubled for second time offenders. While such heavy penalties are seldom, if ever levied, it does stress the importance the Federal Government places on the regulation of such substances. Penalties associated with the illegal use of Schedules III and IV drugs are progressively less, but still enough to serve as potential deterrents.

While no other classification of drugs matches the scope and degree of control found in the federal plan, they do appear to serve more effectively the needs of specific interest groups. One such classification is based upon the clinical and therapeutic use of drugs, which we will examine next.

Drug Use Classification

Many professionals prefer to classify drugs according to how they are used in the treatment of various disorders. While this system is far from perfect, no other system enjoys such wide acceptance within the medical profession. Such a classification includes the following five categories of drugs:

Psychostimulants (sometimes also referred to as stimulants): such drugs, in low to moderate doses, increase alertness, reduce fatigue and elevate mood in most individuals.

Antidepressants: such drugs are used to treat severe, unremitting cases of depression, generally in those instances where no clear cause can be identified. They are not particularly useful in instances where depression is accompanied by mania (a mood swing in the opposite direction).

Anxiolytics (anti-anxiety drugs): such drugs are used in treating disorders where the predominant symptom is anxiety. Because of their general relaxing properties, many drugs in this category can also be used to treat convulsions and to facilitate sleep. The term minor tranquilizer is also sometimes used to describe drugs in this category.

Antipsychotics (neuroleptics): such drugs are used in the treatment of major mental disturbances such as schizophrenia. Because these drugs may calm highly-excited psychotic patients, they are also referred to as major tranquilizers.

Sedative-hypnotics (sometimes referred to as depressants): such drugs are used to calm or relax people at low doses and at higher doses, to induce sleep. However, the hypnotic effect of these drugs (sleep-inducing effect) has nothing to do with the state of hypnosis. Many of these drugs are useful in preparing a patient for surgery as well as serving as anesthetics during surgery.

It is of particular interest to note that the present classification of drugs cuts across Schedules II through IV of the federal classification and reflects a very different focus. Whereas the federal classification reflects a primary concern with the abuse and dependence potential of drugs, the present system reflects a concern for the utility and beneficial effects of drugs. The federal classification, because of the penalties associated with illegal use of drugs, also reflects a more punitive posture while the present classification reflects a more positive image associated with therapeutic potential.

It is also of interest to note that the present classification of drugs makes no mention of illicit (illegal) drugs. This should not be too surprising, since the primary focus of the medical profession is not on illicit drugs but on drugs that facilitate patient treatment. An expansion of the present classification to include illicit drugs would alter the focus considerably. The focus would no longer be primarily on the utility of drugs but rather on the psychological effects of drugs.

Because drugs included in the present classification are controlled by prescription practices, they were dealt with more extensively in the chapter on prescription drugs. At that time, more detail was given, as well as specific examples of drugs provided.

Additional Classification Principles

In addition to the above more formal classifications, drugs are also grouped according to the following categories:

By origin: An example of this category would be drugs that come from plants such as the opium poppy. Categorizing drugs by their source of origin not only recognizes the fact that many drugs of abuse come from plants but also reflects the growing interest in herbal (plant) medicine. Some individuals see this as a viable alternative to traditional medicine.

By similarity of effect: An example of this category would be drugs that have the same effect on heart rate. If two drugs both increase heart rate, they would be grouped together on the basis of such a common property

By chemical structure: For example, the synthetic compounds phenobarbital, amytal and seconal have very similar structures which forms the basis for the category of barbiturate drugs.

By site of action: Certain drugs are classified as central nervous system depressants because of their common, quieting effect on the brain. Conversely, other drugs are categorized as central nervous system stimulants because of their common arousal action on the brain. Drugs that differ widely in some respects may have similar effects on the brain.

By street name: The grouping of drugs in this category has its origin in the subculture and illicit drug market of our society. Examples of such practices would include "speed" (amphetamine compound) and "crack" (a form of cocaine). While such names may be strange to the average person, they serve an essential role in communication on the street. Additional street names of commonly abused drugs are provided in Appendix C.

One final example of a drug category would include the grouping of alcohol and tobacco by themselves. While these two drugs have different pharmacological effects, they share certain perceptions by the public. Both are viewed by the public as not really being drugs at all with such a view frequently reinforced by the media. Thus, it might be more appropriate to simply classify them as unrecognized drugs. As was indicated by a discussion of alcohol and tobacco in Chapter 13, the author favors such a designation.

Concluding Comments

In many respects, classifying drugs is like slicing a cake. One person chooses to cut it in smaller pieces while another person cuts it in larger pieces. Someone else comes along and slices it in a most unconventional way—in layers. We react by saying, "What a strange way to divide a cake." However, they like their cake cut that way and end up eating it as we do. Still someone else comes along and eats the frosting off the top, and we say, "That's not fair, you have to take some cake, too." They respond by saying, "You eat what you want and I'll do the same." Regardless of which of these approaches one uses, it serves the purpose of the consumer. So it is with drug classification also.

One final point regarding the classification of drugs. While all of the previous classifications have merit, the author has chosen to classify drugs on the basis of four major categories: prescription drugs, OTC drugs, illicit drugs and unrecognized drugs (Chapters 10-13). Although such a classification cuts across several of those mentioned in this section, it is less constrained than most.

Hopefully, this has enabled the reader to focus more sharply on matters of personal responsibility in the use of drugs, rather than on more technical and theoretical distinctives.

Note

For more information on drug classification, the reader is referred to: David Grilly. *Drugs and Human Behavior* (Boston: Allyn and Bacon, 1989), Chapter 7; and Tibor Palfai and Henry Jankeiwicz. *Drugs and Human Behavior* (Dubuque, IA: Wm. C. Brown, Publ., 1991), Chapter 13.

Appendix C

List of Street Drugs

Drug	Street Names
Amphetamines	Speed, Uppers, Crank, Pep Pills
Amphetamine Designer Drugs—	
	MDMA, Ecstacy, Adam, Essence, DOM
Amyl Nitrate	Poppers, Snappers
Barbiturates	Blue or Red Devils, Yellow Jacket
Chlorohydrocarbons	Aerosol Sprays, Cleaning Fluids
Cocaine	Coke, Snow, Big C, Lady, Snowbirds
Crack Cocaine	Crack, Rock, Freebase
Hashish	Hash, Hash Oil
Heroin	Smack, Horse, Mud, Big H
Heroin Designer Drugs	MPTP, Synthetic Heroin
Lysergic Acid Diethylamide (LSD)—	
	Acid, Microdot, Sugar Cubes
Marijuana	Pot, Reefer, Grass, Weed, Mary Jane
Mescaline and Peyote	Mesc, Buttons, Cactus
Methaqualone	Quaaludes, Ludes, Sopors
Nitrous Oxide	Laughing Gas, Whippets
Phencyclidine (PCP)	Angel Dust, Hog, Loveboat

Notes

Chapter One

1. Kim Lawton. Churches Enlist in the War on Drugs. *Christianity Today,* February 11, 1991, pp. 44-49.

2. Stephen Arterburn & Jim Burns. *Drug Proof Your Kids* (Pomona, CA: Focus on the Family Pub., 1989), p. 5.

3. Robert Mathias. Marijuana and Tobacco Use Up Again Among 8th and 10th Graders. *NIDA Notes,* March/April, 1997, pp. 12-13.

4. Chris Lutes. *What Teenagers Say About Drugs and Alcohol* (Grand Rapids, MI: Zondervan Pub., Campus Life Books, 1990), p. 79.

5. Frank Minirth, Paul Meier, Siegfried Fink, Walter Byrd & Don Hawkins. *Taking Control* (Grand Rapids, MI: Baker Book House, 1988), pp. 19-20.

6. Ibid.

7. See: Tim Stafford, The Hidden Gospel of the 12 Steps; & Michael Maudlin, Addicts in the Pew, appearing in *Christianity Today,* July 22, 1991, pp. 14-21.

8. Arterburn & Burns, p. 5.

9. Ibid., p. 7.

10. One good additional source of information on numerous drugs is: Frank Minirth, Paul Meier, & Stephen Arterburn. *Miracle Drugs* (Nashville, TN: Thomas Nelson Pub.,1995). Another valuable source is: *Growing Up Drug Free: A Parent's Guide to Prevention* (Washington, DC: U.S. Department of

Education). To order copies of this guide, call the toll-free number (1-800-624-0100).

Chapter Two

1. For example, see article by Will Geisler appearing in *The Chimes*, (Student newspaper, Biola University, November 3, 1995), p. 4.

2. Jason White. *Drug Dependence* (Englewood Cliffs, NJ: Prentice Hall, 1991), p. 7.

3. Stephen Arterburn. *Growing Up Addicted* (New York: Ballantine Books, 1987), pp. 49-67.

4. Oakley Ray and Charles Ksir. *Drugs, Society & Human Behavior*, 5th. Ed. (St. Louis: Times Mirror/Mosby, 1990), p. 13.

5. Ibid., p. 17.

6. Richard Fields. *Drugs and Alcohol in Perspective* (Dubuque, IA: Wm. C. Brown, Pub., 1992), pp. 13-14.

7. Ray and Ksir, p. 18.

8. Joel Robertson. *Kids Don't Want to Use Drugs* (Nashville, TN: Thomas Nelson, Pub., 1992), pp. 103-112.

9. Ray and Ksir, p. 8.

10. Stephen Maisto, Mark Galizio, and Gerard Connors. *Drug Use and Misuse* (Fort Worth, TX: Holt, Rinehart and Winston, 1991), p. 328.

11. Ray and Ksir, p. 8.

12. Robert Morey. *How to Keep your Kids Drug Free* (Eugene, OR: Harvest House Pub., 1993), p. 9.

Chapter Three

1. Tibor Palfai and Henry Jankiewicz. *Drugs and Human Behavior* (Dubuque, IA.: Wm. C. Brown Pub., 1991), p. 5.

2. Ibid.

3. *The New International Dictionary of the Bible* (Grand Rapids, MI: Zondervan Pub. House, 1987), p. 801.

4. Palfai and Jankiewicz, p. 422.

5. *Young's Analytical Concordance to the Bible* (Nashville, TN: Thomas Nelson Pub., 1982), p. 916.

6. Ibid.

7. Palfai and Jankiewicz, p. 4.

8. Comments accompanying passage in *The New Student Bible*, NIV (Grand Rapids, MI.: Zondervan Pub. House, 1992), p. 456.

9. *The New International Dictionary of the Bible*, p. 805.

10. Ibid., pp. 799, 806.

11. *Baker's Encyclopedia of the Bible*, Vol. 2 (Grand Rapids, MI.: Baker Book House, 1988), pp. 1728-1729.

12. *New Bible Dictionary*, 2nd Ed. (Wheaton, IL.: Tyndale House Pub. Inc., 1982), p. 946.

13. *Baker's Encyclopedia of the Bible*, pp. 1722-1723.

Chapter Four

1. Claude A. Villee. *Biology*, 6th Ed. (Philadelphia: W. B. Saunders Co., 1972), p. 349.

2. Matthew Henry. *A Commentary on the Whole Bible*, Vol. 6. (Iowa Falls, IA.: World Bible Publishers), p. 742.

3. Introduction to I Corinthians in *The New Student Bible*, NIV. (Grand Rapids, MI.: Zondervan Pub. House, 1992), p. 1020.

4. Holy Health (Interview of David Larson by Christopher A. Hall). *Christianity Today,* 23 Nov., 1992, pp. 18-22.

5. Ibid.

6. Ibid.

7. Ibid.

8. Ibid.

9. Matthew Henry, Vol. 6, p. 820.

10. Jason M. White. *Drug Dependence* (Englewood Cliffs, NJ: Prentice Hall, 1991), p. 6.

11. Ibid., p.208.

12. Ibid., p. 220.

13. Ibid.

14. Such experimental drugs as AZT do not provide a cure for AIDS but merely slow down the progress of symptoms. Some of the more recent "protease inhibitor" drugs (e.g., ritonavir) have proven to be even more effective in delaying the progression of symptoms, particularly when combined with AZT (cocktail treatment).

15 Robert Morey. *How To Keep Your Kids Drug Free* (Eugene, OR: Harvest House Pub., 1993), p. 25.

Chapter Five

1. James Kalat. *Biological Psychology*, 4th Ed. (Belmont, CA.: Wadsworth Pub. Co., 1992), p. 87.

2. Oakley Ray and Charles Ksir. *Drugs, Society, and Human Behavior,* 5th Ed. (St. Louis: Times Mirror/Mosby, 1990), p. 296.

3. Kalat, p. 491.

4. It is important to avoid the dualistic pitfall of the mind-body problem. To consider the mind as part of the body and having control over it is consistent with Scriptural teachings.

5. Matthew Henry. *A Commentary on the Whole Bible*, Vol. 5 (Iowa Falls, IA.: World Bible Pub.) p. 325.

6. Kim A. Lawton. Churches Enlist in the War on Drugs. *Christianity Today*, 11 Feb. 1991, pp. 44-49.

7. Robert Morey. *How To Keep Your Kids Drug Free* (Eugene, OR.: Harvest House Pub., 1993), p. 57.

8. Ibid., p. 55.

9. Harry Avis. *Drugs and Life* (Dubuque, IA.: Wm. C. Brown Pub., 1990), p. 254. For a personal account of the effects of mescaline (the most active chemical in the peyote plant), the reader is referred to: Aldous Huxley, *The Doors of Perception* (New York: Harper and Brothers, 1954).

10. Ray and Ksir, p. 295.

Chapter Six

1. Tim Stafford. The Therapeutic Revolution. *Christianity Today*, 17 May 1993, pp. 24-32.

2. Merrill F. Unger. *Demons in the World Today* (Wheaton, IL.: Tyndale House, 1988), pp. 130-131.

3. Ibid., p. 126.

4. Ibid., p. 131.

5. Charles E. Hummel. *The Prosperity Gospel* (Downers Grove, IL.: Inter Varsity Press, 1991).

6. Ibid., p. 12.

7. Ibid., p. 14.

8. Ibid., p. 8.

9. Ibid., pp. 13-14.

10. Ibid., p. 20.

11. James R. Goff, Jr. The Faith That Claims. *Christianity Today*, 19 Feb. 1990, p. 21.

12. Hummel, p. 26.

13. Ibid., p. 20.

14. Ibid., p. 15.

15. Elliot Miller. The Christian, Energetic Medicine, New Age Paranoia. *Christian Research Journal,* Winter, 1992, pp. 24-27.

16. Oakley Ray and Charles Ksir. *Drugs, Society, and Human Behavior,* 5th. Ed. (St. Louis: Times Mirror/Mosby, 1990), pp. 253-254.

17. Unger, p. 132.

Chapter Seven

1. David Myers. *Psychology*, 3rd. Ed. (New York: Worth Pub., 1992), p. 100.

2. Charles M. Shelton. *Morality of the Heart* (New York: Crossroad Pub. Co., 1990), p. 27.

3. Note on Rom. 13:1 in *The New Student Bible,* NIV (Grand Rapids, MI.: Zondervan Pub. House, 1992), p. 1017.

4. For an interesting discussion of civil disobedience from a Christian perspective, read Chapters 7 & 8 in Francis A. Schaeffer's book, *A Christian Manifesto* (Westchester, IL.: Crossway Books, 1981).

5. Oakley Ray & Charles Ksir. *Drugs, Society, & Human Behavior,* 5th Ed. (St. Louis: Times Mirror/Mosby, 1990), pp. 44-45.

6. Ibid., p. 49.

7. Ibid., p. 52.

8. Weldon Witters, Peter Venturelli, & Glen Hanson. *Drugs and Society,* 3rd. Ed. (Boston: Jones and Bartlett Pub., 1992), pp. 73-75.

9. See Stephen Arterburn. *Growing Up Addicted* (New York: Ballantine Books, 1987), pp. 49-67 and James Kalat, *Biological Psychology,* 5th Ed. (Pacific Grove, CA.: Brooks/Cole Pub. Co., 1995), p. 91.

10. Ray & Ksir, pp. 52-56.

11. Ibid., pp. 335-336.

12. Ibid., p. 341.

13. Ibid., p. 342.

14. The voter's approval of Proposition 215 (legalization of marijuana for medical use) in California has only further complicated the issue. However, federal law supersedes state law and marijuana's legal status remains the same.

Chapter Eight

1. Frank Minirth, Paul Meier, Siegfried Fink, Walter Byrd, and Don Hawkins. *Taking Control* (Grand Rapids, MI: Baker Book House, 1988), p. 121.

2. Note on Prov. 22:6 in *The New Student Bible,* NIV (Grand Rapids, MI: Zondervan Pub. House, 1992), p. 586.

3. Joel C. Robertson. *Kids Don't Want to Use Drugs* (Nashville, TN: Thomas Nelson Pub., 1992), p. 75.

4. Ibid., p. 76.

5. Chris Lutes. *What Teenagers Are Saying About Drugs and Alcohol* (Grand Rapids, MI: Zondervan Pub. House, 1990), p. 134.

6. Ibid.

7. Minirth, et al., p. 123. These authors report that the father was absent or a peripheral figure in two-thirds of the families with a drug-abusing child.

8. Ibid.

9. While the term "normal" implies consistency over time, some degree of flexibility in the behavior of teenagers should be expected and accepted without it being viewed as deviant.

10. Some symptoms of drug abuse followed by withdrawal symptoms may be characterized by such an "on and off" picture.

11. Robertson, pp. 142-143.

12. While drug abuse must, at some point, be recognized as sin, one should not overly emphasize this point at the expense of other damaging effects of abuse.

Chapter Nine

1. For a discussion of the use of controlled drinking as a solution to alcoholism see: Richard Fields. *Drugs and Alcohol in Perspective* (Dubuque, IA: Wm. C. Brown, Pub., 1992), pp. 326-327; and Harry Avis. *Drugs and Life* (Dubuque, IA: Wm. C. Brown, Pub., 1990), p. 385.

2. David M. Grilly. *Drugs and Human Behavior* (Boston: Allyn & Bacon, 1989), p. 153.

3. Fields, pp. 304-305.

4. Ibid., p. 306.

5. Oakley Ray and Charles Ksir. *Drugs, Society, & Human Behavior,* 5th Ed. (St. Louis: Times Mirror/Mosby, 1990), pp. 361-362.

6. Ibid., p. 181. Withdrawal symptoms from alcohol are extremely dangerous and can be life threatening.

7. Ibid., pp. 367-369.

8. Tim Stafford. The Hidden Gospel of the 12 Steps. *Christianity Today*, 22 July 1991, pp. 14-19.

9. This group is not to be confused with the Anglo-Catholic Oxford Movement associated with John Henry Newman.

10. Frank Minirth, Paul Meier, Siegfried Fink, Walter Byrd, and Don Hawkins. Taking Control (Grand Rapids, MI: Baker Book House, 1988), pp. 99-115.

11. Robert S. McGee, Pat Springle, and Susan Joiner. *Rapha's 12-Step Program for Overcoming Chemical Dependency,* 2nd. Ed. (Houston, TX: Rapha Publishing/Word, Inc., 1990).

12. For further information write to: Overcomers Outreach, Inc., 2290 W. Whittier Blvd., Suite D, La Habra, CA 90631.

13. Minirth, et al., p. 97.

Chapter Ten

1. An exception to this rule has been made by the Federal Government in permitting a small drug company, Uni-Med, Inc., to produce Marinol (a capsule containing marijuana) for the purpose of reducing nausea associated with cancer chemotherapy.

2. Harry Avis. *Drugs and Life* (Dubuque, IA.: Wm. C. Brown, Pub., 1990), p. 332.

3. *Diagnostic and Statistical Manual of Mental Disorders*, 4th. Ed. (Washington, D. C.: American Psychiatric Association, 1994).

4. Avis, p. 331.

5. *Diagnostic and Statistical Manual of Mental Disorders*, pp. 78-85.

6. Oakley Ray and Charles Ksir. *Drugs, Society, and Human Behavior,* 5th. Ed. (St. Louis: Times Mirror/Mosby, 1990), p. 140.

7. Lawrence D. Chilnick, Bert Stern, Harold M. Silverman, and Gilbert I. Simon. *The Pill Book,* 7th. Ed. (New York: Bantam Books, 1996), pp. 1213-1216.

8. Ibid.

9. James W. Kalat. *Biological Psychology,* 5th Ed. (Pacific Grove, CA: Brooks/Cole Pub. Co., 1995), p. 420.

10. Ibid., p. 396.

11. Wayne A. Payne, Dale B. Hahn, and Robert R. Pinger. *Drugs: Issues for Today* (St. Louis: Mosby Year Book, 1991), pp. 95, 106.

12. Arthur P. Leccese. *Drugs and Society: Behavioral Medicines and Abusable Drugs* (Englewood Cliffs, NJ: Prentice Hall, 1991), p. 76.

Chapter Eleven

1. Oakley Ray & Charles Ksir. *Drugs, Society, & Human Behavior,* 5th Ed. (St. Louis: Times Mirror/Mosby, 1990), pp. 234-236.

2. Ibid.

3. Harry Avis. *Drugs & Life* (Dubuque, IA.: W. C. Brown, Pub., 1990), pp. 298-299.

4. Ray & Ksir, pp. 237-238.

5. Ibid.

6. Ibid.

7. James W. Kalat. *Biological Psychology*, 5th Ed. (Pacific Grove, CA.: Brooks/Cole Pub. Co., 1995), p. 367.

8. Alan F. Schatzberg & Jonathan O. Cole. *Manual of Clinical Psychopharmacology,* 2nd. Ed. (Washington, D. C.: American Psychiatric Press, Inc., 1991), p. 243.

9. Ray & Ksir, p. 248.

10. Charles B. Clayman, ed., *The American Medical Association Guide to Prescription and Over-The-Counter Drugs* (New York: Random House, 1988), p. 434.

11. Ray & Ksir, p. 249. While these authors also include caffeine as one of the common ingredients found in OTC cold remedies, caffeine has been deleted in the present list because of its widespread presence in many non-drug products.

12. In many instances, the consumer may save 30-40% by choosing the drug-store generic form of an OTC product.

Chapter Twelve

1. Oakley Ray and Charles Ksir. *Drugs, Society, and Human Behavior*, 5th. Ed. (St Louis: Times Mirror/Mosby, 1990), p. 83.

2. Ronald K. Siegel. Changing patterns of cocaine use: Longitudinal observations, consequences, and treatment. In J. Grabowski, ed. *Cocaine: Pharmacology, Effects, and Treatment of Abuse. NIDA Research Monograph 50* (Rockville, MD.: U. S. Department of Health and Human Services, 1984).

3. Ray and Ksir, p. 126.

4. Ibid., p. 125.

5. While the federal government and other officials refer to many drugs as narcotics, the designation correctly applies only to those drugs that are opiates—natural or synthetic.

6. See Ray and Ksir, p. 292 and Stephen A. Maisto, Mark Galizio and Gerald J. Connors. *Drug Use and Misuse* (Fort Worth, TX: Holt, Rinehart and Winston, Inc., 1991), p. 274.

7. Tibor Palfai and Henry Jankiewicz. *Drugs and Human Behavior* (Dubuque, IA: Wm. C. Brown, Pub., 1991), p. 438.

8. Ray and Ksir, p. 303.

9. Ibid., p. 314.

10. Ibid., pp. 324-325.

11. Wayne A. Payne, Dale B. Hahn and Robert R. Pinger. *Drugs: Issues for Today* (St. Louis, MO.: Mosby Year Book, Inc., 1991), p. 263.

12. Ibid.

13. In general, marijuana increases the heart rate and makes the heart work harder in order to maintain blood circulation. These effects are similar to those of stress.

14. Ray and Ksir, p. 384.

15. This tragedy is reported in numerous sources. For one such account see: Maisto, et al., p. 67.

16. Welden Witters, Peter Venturelli, and Glen Hanson. *Drugs and Society,* 3rd Ed. (Boston: Jones and Bartlett Pub., 1992), pp. 349-350.

Chapter Thirteen

1. Prohibition (the prevention of the manufacturing, distribution and sale of alcoholic beverages) was enacted by the 18th Amendment to the U. S. Constitution on January 16, 1920. Because of the illegal buying and selling of alcohol and the inability of the federal government to enforce the ruling, prohibition was repealed by the 21st Amendment on February 20, 1933.

2. The first warning labels on cigarette packages were required by the federal government on January 1, 1966.

3. While most states use a BAL of 0.10 as a legal definition of intoxication, some states have even more rigorous standards. In California, a BAL of 0.08 is now considered legal intoxication. A similar reduction in the legal definition of intoxication may soon be mandated for all states by the federal government.

4. Oakley Ray and Charles Ksir. *Drugs, Society & Human Behavior,* 5th Ed. (St Louis: Times Mirror/Mosby, 1990), p. 172.

5. Ibid., p. 174.

6. Ibid., p. 173.

7. Ibid., p. 178.

8. Richard Fields. *Drugs and Alcohol in Perspective* (Dubuque, IA: Wm. C. Brown Pub., 1992), p. 14.

9. Ray & Ksir, p. 190

10. Ibid., p. 195

11. Ibid., p. 212.

12. Ibid., p. 205.

13. Ibid., pp. 202-203.

14. Lauran Neergaard. Cigarettes found to steal time from smoker's life. *Orange County Register,* Santa Ana, CA, 27 August, 1993, p. 24.

15. Ray & Ksir, p. 204.

16. Tibor Palfai and Henry Jankiewicz. *Drugs and Human Behavior* (Dubuque, IA: Wm. C. Brown Pub. 1991), p. 349.

17. Ray & Ksir, p. 200.

18. Palfai & Jankeiwicz, p. 348.